creating the
EFFECTIVE
PRIMARY SCHOOL

creating the

EFFECTIVE
PRIMARY SCHOOL

a guide for school leaders and teachers

ROGER SMITH

P^{TES}rimary

Inspiration for teachers

**KOGAN
PAGE**

First published in 2002

Kogan Page Limited
120 Pentonville Road
London N1 9JN
UK

Stylus Publishing Inc
22883 Quicksilver Drive
Sterling VA 20166-2012
USA

British Library Cataloguing in Publication Data

A CIP record for this book is available from the British Library.

ISBN 0 7494 3538 0

Typeset by JS Typesetting, Wellingborough, Northants
Printed and bound in Great Britain by Clays Ltd, St Ives plc

CONTENTS

INTRODUCTION

Creating an effective school is very much like travelling on a long journey. When Christopher Columbus set off on his epic voyage, he didn't really know where he was going; when he arrived, he didn't really know where he was; and when he returned home he wasn't all that clear just exactly where he had been. Schools can't function like that because children deserve success as soon as they enter their first classroom and this success needs to continue. This means that schools do need to know where they are going, what they are aiming for, and when they have completed one part of the process successfully they need to understand what they did and how they did it so that the success can be repeated.

An effective school will only exist if all those who have a role to play within it know what to do to make it effective and how to do it well. Headteachers and senior teachers will have to organise, lead and manage the school successfully as well as 'selling' it to parents in a way that encourages and develops excellent teaching and learning. All the pupils will have to progress and achieve in line with their abilities and those involved indirectly in the day-to-day workings of the school such as governors and parents will have to be supportive and, where necessary, act as a critical friend. The school will have to market itself as a centre of excellence and as it does so it will have that certain culture and ethos which, while difficult to define, keeps saying to anyone with an interest in the school that this is a positive, hard-working centre of educational excellence. Last, but certainly not least, an effective school will be seen as effective by external inspection and the public will know of its effectiveness and success through the publication of the inspection report and any subsequent positive reports in local newspapers.

In other words, everyone has to do their job well because no one who works in schools wants to be thought of as ineffective and no teacher, headteacher, governor, parent or child wants their school to be seen as under-performing and unsuccessful. One excellent teacher in a mediocre school will not make the school effective but one bad teacher in an otherwise successful school will bring down its level of effectiveness significantly. Everyone will have to work together to achieve high standards.

If schools are to continue to promote and ensure high quality learning, they have to develop effective strategies. What these are can be elusive and difficult to define. When members of the committee who later produced the Elton Report (1989) visited schools, they were able to see all kinds of variations in 'feel' or 'atmosphere' and they were convinced that some schools were more effective than others because: 'some schools [had] a more positive atmosphere than others' (1989: 88). The report, which concentrated on the state of 'discipline' in schools, was actually much more wide ranging and suggested, in its conclusions, that a whole variety of people affected how successful a school was. They ranged from parents to all pupils and all teachers, and a shared commitment to education was one of the keys to a school's success.

It is important as a starting point for me to suggest some of these basic issues which, when taken together, describe what actually needs to happen to a school to make it successful and effective. These characteristics of an effective school will include:

❑ good leadership offering breadth of vision and the ability to motivate others;
❑ appropriate delegation with involvement in policy making by staff other than the head;
❑ clearly established staffing structures;
❑ well-qualified staff with expertise and experience;
❑ clear aims and objectives;
❑ effective communication and clear systems of record keeping and assessment;
❑ the means and ability to develop pupils' particular strengths and to promote high expectations;
❑ a coherent curriculum;
❑ a positive ethos with an orderly yet relaxed working atmosphere;
❑ a suitable working environment;
❑ appropriate deployment of staff and materials;
❑ good relationships with parents, governors and the local community;
❑ the capacity to manage change and solve problems.

To reiterate: successful schools do not just happen. They don't just exist and continue to exist by waving a magic wand. They require hard work and systematic planning. Each chapter of this book will make the move towards excellence in schools easier to achieve and will summarise issues that are important in helping us to recognise all the factors that lead to successful schools. In addition, in some chapters and some sections within chapters there are useful lists and suggested activities, which can be used in staff development with teachers and, occasionally, teaching assistants.

The chapters are as follows:

- **Chapter 1 – The organisation of the school: creating a positive ethos** examines how the organisation of the school creates a positive ethos. It considers aims statements, management structures and the organisation of schools, school atmosphere, leadership, and communication, including key documents.
- **Chapter 2 – Relationships in the school** looks at relationships and how teams are built. It discusses decision making, the kinds of positive relationships that help teachers work together and how to resolve any conflicts between adults who work in school.
- **Chapter 3 – The curriculum and raising pupil achievement** is concerned with the curriculum and raising pupil achievement. The curriculum is identified and there are suggestions as to how the curriculum can be planned.
- **Chapter 4 – Target setting and raising achievement** recognises how important targets are in planning to raise achievement.
- **Chapter 5 – Successful teaching and effective classroom management** recognises that successful teaching and classroom management is important and examines assertive teaching, effective classroom relationships and general strategies for successful teaching.
- **Chapter 6 – Accountability and the inspection process** deals with the inspection process and how it can improve schools. It concentrates on the impact of OFSTED and looks at what a school can do before the inspection as well as how the inspection process can move the school forward. There are also sections on what OFSTED actually expect an effective school to look like.
- **Chapter 7 – Performance management and the successful school** discusses performance management and recognises that the effective school will play a key role in school improvement. It looks at the performance management cycle and suggests various strategies that will make it more effective in your school.
- **Chapter 8 – Stress management and time management** deals with what are, unfortunately, symptoms of our time, which can affect teachers in ways that make what they and the school do less effective. There are suggestions in this chapter on how to limit stress and how teachers can manage their time more efficiently.

THE ORGANISATION OF THE SCHOOL: CREATING A POSITIVE ETHOS

This chapter looks at:

❑ organisation of the school;
❑ ways of organising the whole school;
❑ organisational structures;
❑ leadership and positive ethos;
❑ leadership styles;
❑ communication.

It considers the importance of school organisation and the ways in which school leaders can organise schools effectively.

INTRODUCTION

It may sound simplistic, but effective schools are vibrant, enthusiastic and ever-changing organisations which don't just suddenly happen; they actually have to be organised. In saying this, it is important that they are organised in such a way that there is a positive ethos and a learning atmosphere where every child succeeds in some way and where every adult works towards helping every child achieve his or her maximum potential. One common assumption about the purpose of schools that we must make is that they should develop the intellectual, social, emotional and physical abilities of all children. This is summarised in Table 1.1. The organisation of the school and how it works effectively will be geared to making sure that these purposes are central to how the school functions.

Table 1.1 *The purpose of schools*

Intellectual purposes – making sure that children of all abilities are learning and that the organisation of the school supports this learning
Social purposes – allowing children to develop socially within a secure and supportive environment
Emotional purposes – providing children with the security within which they can overcome any doubts about their own ability and self-esteem and succeed in whatever they want to do
Physical purposes – allowing children time and space to be able to manipulate their physical world, which can range from learning to manipulate a pair of scissors to learning to swim

ORGANISATION OF THE SCHOOL

The successful organisation of the school is really about managing all the diverse attitudes of the people that are involved in the process of running it day by day and year by year into something coherent and shared. This does not mean creating a situation in which everyone holds the same views or in which there is no disagreement about the nature of how to manage the organisation, although there is little doubt that, in effective schools, staff share an ability to work together towards a set of clearly understood purposes which are seen as reasonable to all those involved.

Managing the organisation of the school in all its complexities and subtleties is unlikely to be carried out effectively by those headteachers and leaders who stick rigidly to a top-down style of management. Success is much more likely to be achieved by using a variety of strategies that involve responding to the different needs of everyone involved.

There are several basic organisational concepts that are, in many ways, the backbone of the whole structure of a school and which need to be referred back to as the building blocks of how the school operates effectively and successfully. Here is a brief résumé of six key concepts.

1. Objectives and aims

It is important to establish an aims statement that drives the school forward and is at the centre of everything that happens in the school. This should be a public statement that everyone is aware of and it should have been developed by all those with a vested interest in the school, including teachers, teaching assistants, parents, governors and, where appropriate, older children. At its core is a statement about what the school is trying to achieve.

There are many statements of intent in a primary school. Many of these relate to the curriculum, teaching, behaviour, anti-bullying, etc, and exist in policies relating to all kinds of subjects as well as in the school prospectus which is a key document for parents. But, all of these must always relate back to the core statement of intent which, as an aims statement, is the heart of what the school actually does. Table 1.2 is an example of a broad aims statement.

Table 1.2 *School aims statement*

The school will commit itself to creating a harmonious and stimulating environment in which all pupils will be encouraged to achieve their maximum potential in terms of skills, knowledge and understanding. Each pupil will be offered opportunities to take decisions, use his or her own judgement, work cooperatively with others and develop as a confident individual. We aim to provide a broad and balanced which incorporates the requirements of the National Curriculum.

---

2. The structure of the school

This is about roles and responsibilities, tasks, areas of work and, in short, who does what, when and how. It is about communicating information, organising tasks, taking decisions and organising who works with whom. Primary schools are full of structures, including class groupings, teams, Key Stage planning teams, coordinators, senior teachers, timetables, etc. Some of these structures are determined externally, such as salary scales and admission policies for LEA schools, and others are decided internally, such as the allocation of posts above the main teachers' pay spine, including management and leadership posts.

3. Leadership

This is about who gets things going, who has responsibility and who offers direction to the school. It will be discussed in more detail later in the chapter.

Usually in primary schools leadership is represented by the headteacher and the deputy headteacher. This has changed radically during the past few years and there are now important management roles allocated to all curriculum coordinators. In the teachers' pay structure there are leadership posts which widen the senior teacher team to include such appointments as assistant headteachers. In fact, in effective schools most adults who work in them, including secretaries, site managers and chairs of governors, have to act as leaders on certain occasions.

4. Power

This is not quite the same as leadership but it is about who has the authority to do things and who is able to use their power positively and who uses it negatively. Power often underpins the role of many leaders. Authority, which on most occasions is legitimate power, might stem from an individual coordinator's expertise in music or technology, for example, or because of age and/or experience. Power can be seen as quite widely distributed, but it has to be said that the principal source of power in the primary school lies in the hands of the headteacher.

5. Ethos

Each school has its own ethos which is determined by its underlying beliefs and values. The ethos or culture of a primary school is usually an amalgamation of social, moral and academic values. These values determine how children relate to each other, how staff and children relate and define relationships in terms of courtesy, care consideration, competition, individuality and mutual dependence, for example. The ethos is also about what is considered right and proper, for example helpfulness, cooperation, respect for others, and what are the beliefs upon which such things as the academic curriculum is based.

6. Environmental relationships

Schools exist in an environment with which they constantly react. They are affected by their context which relates to the school type, its catchment area, the LEA, types of governors and the demands of central government and national policy.

7

In the rest of this chapter the brief descriptions of the 'building blocks' of school organisation outlined above are used as the basis for a closer investigation of what constitutes good organisation in primary schools. First of all, let's look more closely at the structure of the school.

Internal and external structures

These are largely the elements and systems that naturally exist in schools and they consist of structures that are either internal or external (see Table 1.3).

Table 1.3 *Internal and external structures that affect the school*

INTERNAL STRUCTURES	EXTERNAL STRUCTURES
Class groupings	Numbers on roll
Subject groups	Admission numbers
Year teams	Salary scales
Departments	School budget
Subject coordinators	Length of the school day
Timetables and room	Governing body
allocation	Performance management
Meetings	National Curriculum, etc
Teams	
Working groups, etc	

Clearly there is a certain amount of interdependency between the two groups of structures. For example, class groupings, and subject groups such as sets for maths, will be dependent on the number of pupils on the school roll and the numbers in particular years. The number of teachers and the number paid above the basic pay spine will be, to a large extent, dependent on the amount of money in the school budget which will itself be dependent in the main on the numbers on roll in the school.

Organisational dimensions

All schools are dependent on teams of individuals. However, individuals cannot work and perform effectively without effective groups or teams within the wider organisation. On this basis the organisation of a school could be represented as shown in Figure 1.1. The links between the

Individual	Group	Organisation
Headteacher	Classes	Nursery schools
Deputy headteacher	Year group	Infants
Teachers and pupils	Key Stages teams	Juniors, etc
Coordinators	Year teams	
Parents	Committees	
Governors	Working parties	
Site manager/caretaker		
Secretary		

Figure 1.1 *The organisational dimension*

individual, the group and the organisation can be extended even further to include LEAs, teacher unions, DfEE and OFSTED.

However far we extend these interrelationships it is important to emphasise one key issue: organisational dimensions of the school are management structures, and managing a school has to be first and foremost about individuals working together. This is where we have to start looking at different ways of organising the whole school.

WAYS OF ORGANISING THE WHOLE SCHOOL

Different types of organisation

Although schools have many similarities each is also unique. It is useful to look at some of the factors which most directly affect particular primary schools.

Size

Larger primary schools will often need a tighter and better-developed structure. They will tend to be more hierarchical and may well have departments, Key Stage teams and year teams that will not be found in smaller primary schools.

Designation

Obviously the title of the school will have considerable impact on how it is organised and what needs to be organised within it. The title is very important, whether it be nursery, infant junior or primary, county, community and/or denominational. Each will have its own influence on what can and cannot happen and what actually needs to take place for the school to be successful.

Leaders and led

All schools are hierarchical to some degree in that there is always a headteacher, teaching and non-teaching staff. In most schools there are deputy headteachers and several teachers may well have management or leadership allowances. Some schools will be very hierarchical, which can produce its own obvious problems. Others will be what is described as collegial. A general guide is that the larger the school, the more hierarchical is its management structure.

Design

School design can have an important impact on how it is organised. Some schools have classrooms that can be closed, while others are more open plan. Some are all on one site and others are split into several buildings. Long corridors, small dining rooms, the lack of sinks and temporary classrooms, for example, can influence what can be achieved relatively easily and what will be difficult to manage.

Culture

The way 'things get done' will affect how the school works, how efficiently it is managed and how adults and children relate to each other. This culture or ethos is often a product of history but it can be influenced by school size, how hierarchical the management style is and how the school is designed.

Cohesion

Any primary school is a mixture of many parts which have to come together in order to work effectively. The extent to which smaller groups and teams join together into a successful whole will influence the success of the school in maintaining and raising achievement, or not.

Hierarchy and collegiality

Where a hierarchical structure dominates, there is likely to be more direction, more control and more commands from the 'top'. The nature of this kind of structure will mean that the power is directed downwards and this will take place largely through a series of instructions with less room for discussion and debate. Although this kind of chain of command does not necessarily stop colleagues from working together, it can also make it more difficult. Collegiality on the other hand is more about professional colleagues cooperating, participating and delegating within a structure where working in decision-making teams is seen as important. The usual hierarchical pyramid looks like the one shown in Figure 1.2. Obviously, in smaller schools the pyramid will be much tighter and in many cases flatter because of the absence of a deputy or senior teachers.

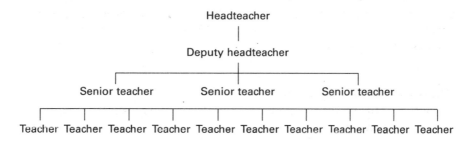

Figure 1.2 *Hierarchical pyramid*

In many small schools a hierarchical structure might be totally inappropriate (in fact it could be suggested that this kind of organisational structure is hardly ever appropriate in a primary school), but it is the case that some schools will be more collegial, some will be more hierarchical and others will be able to successfully combine the two. They will all, however, be organised in a way that aims to achieve effective results and to maintain good relationships between those who work in them.

Results versus relationships

Most organisations face a problem in striking a balance between achieving results and maintaining good relationships between those who work in the organisation. Schools are no different and it is often difficult to be both concerned about results and people.

There are basically three sets of needs that any manager has to consider. They are:

- ❑ what tasks need completing to achieve results;
- ❑ the needs of the staff team;
- ❑ the needs of the individual staff member.

11

Unfortunately, these three needs do not remain static but shift and change in terms of priority. Whatever type of structure you think would work best in your situation, it is important to determine where your school stands on a results–relationship continuum. Tannenbaum and Schmidt (1973) suggest that this kind of continuum has at its two extremes an autocratic and a democratic structure (Figure 1.3).

Results Relationships

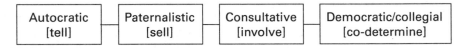

| Autocratic [tell] | Paternalistic [sell] | Consultative [involve] | Democratic/collegial [co-determine] |

Figure 1.3 *The results relationship continuum*

Processes will take place somewhere on this continuum. In many schools, individuals and teams will operate at one or several stages of the continuum.

Tell or talk

At the autocratic end, *telling* is the favoured method that managers use to organise what happens in the school. Orders are given and the expectation is that they are carried out. As we move along the continuum, the stages involve increasing amounts of dialogue as there has to be an attempt by managers such as heads and deputies to *sell* ideas to colleagues by persuading them to accept them. Involving colleagues, however, is more about heads and deputies consulting them about new ideas, changes in direction and different ways of working. It is this kind of *consultation* that marks a halfway point between autocracy and democracy. At the end of the continuum the management processes and the structures that are in place must recognise consensus as an effective way of both getting results and meeting the needs of people. Colleagues need to be able to *co-determine* what happens in the school through the use of teams of teachers and decision-making meetings.

School atmosphere

The perceptive but largely neglected Elton Report (1989), which was mentioned briefly in the introduction, includes the nebulous but useful phrase 'school atmosphere' (1989: 89). The report emphasises that there were 'differences in their [schools] feel or atmosphere' (1989: 88), and that 'perhaps the most important characteristic of schools with a positive atmosphere is that pupils teachers and other staff feel that they are known and valued members of the school community' (1989: 90). The Report goes on to suggest that schools with a negative atmosphere suffer more from bad behaviour than those with a positive atmosphere. This predictable and obvious conclusion nevertheless is vitally important, not least because creating a positive atmosphere and developing an effective ethos is extremely hard and involves commitment and time from headteachers, teachers, parents, governors and pupils. One way of considering what we don't want in our schools is to consider those symptoms which suggest a negative atmosphere so that we can work hard to stop them happening. They will include: litter; graffiti; late arrivals; teachers starting lessons late or finishing lessons early; ignoring bad behaviour; high absence rate; work not marked; work not displayed; inappropriate punishments . . . the list can go on and on.

Many of these negative symptoms reflect how the school functions as a community and, more generally, a negative atmosphere suggests a failure to achieve any sense of communal coherence. By extension, a school with a negative atmosphere will not be an effective school and it will probably mean that staff and pupils are undervalued and teacher expectations may well be low. If this is the case then there has to be radical change in the way staff and children value the school as a community. The management functions that are necessary to effect these changes (and many of them form part of later sections of this book) might include the quality of the leadership; classroom management; behaviour management; the curriculum and how it is organised and taught; pastoral care; buildings and the physical environment; and relationships with parents and governors. In other words, a wide range of tasks and issues.

The organisational culture of the school

The culture of the school is much easier to demonstrate than the more vague concept of atmosphere, although it has to be said that the initial feeling of atmosphere parents get when they enter a school will often dominate their ideas about whether it is suitable for their child. Culture, however, is about the implicit and explicit values that govern the way people in the school interact. It is people who create the school culture but it is affected by several other factors, for example:

❑ Split-site schools, and schools with separate buildings, will influence how often staff meet and how often they are able to talk to each other, learn from each other and work alongside each other in professional teams.

❏ The ways in which staff interact socially will have a bearing on how they work together. Who meets with whom at break times, lunchtime and after school will affect working patterns in terms of who is likely to work together as a team.

❏ A school's history and traditions affect and go some way to explain staff and pupil behaviour. What has been tried in the past, crises that have been survived and all kinds of adversities that have been overcome will have an influence on present behaviour.

❏ There are rituals and ceremonies which are often linked to eating and drinking: tea and coffee arrangements; who brings biscuits; who meets in the pub; and what happens when someone leaves.

All these, and more, will contribute to the overall culture of how the school works. However rigorously schools are structured and planned, it is ultimately how the people inside them interact, and what they value and believe in, that makes a good school distinctive and vibrant.

ORGANISATIONAL STRUCTURES

It is also important to recognise that in order for a school to be effective there has to be a strong organisational structure. It is within this organisational culture that people work together under the umbrella of strong and effective leadership (Table 1.4). This is discussed in more detail in Smith's *Successful School Management*, Cassell (1998).

LEADERSHIP AND POSITIVE ETHOS

Effective leadership tends to produce a positive atmosphere and a sense of security. However, linking leadership to the culture of the school is difficult and the easiest way to do this is to look at two related aspects: the personal qualities needed to manage adults, and the actual management style. Both concepts will be looked at in more detail later in this chapter, but whatever role is assumed, it will be important because it is central to creating the kind of positive ethos that will improve learning. When headteachers, teachers and coordinators are taking charge of some aspect of the running of the school, they should have an awareness of pupils' needs and be a curriculum leader as well as a forward planner. They will need to manage resources well, and communicate their ideas to everyone who has an interest

Table 1.4 *Effective schools and organisational culture*

CHARACTERISTICS OF EFFECTIVE SCHOOLS	CHARACTERISTICS OF STRONG ORGANISATIONAL CULTURES
Coherent ethos with agreed ways of doing things	Strong culture with shared values and a consensus on 'how we do things around here'
Importance of leadership	Importance of a strong leader who embodies core values and who finds other leaders with similar values
Strong beliefs about teaching and learning	Widely shared beliefs that are reflected in common practices and rituals
Teachers act as role models	All employees represent core values to the children
Staff training influences what happens in the school	Staff see training as renewing their attempts to create and maintain an effective school
There are effective meetings with joint planning and problem solving.	Core values are constantly reinforced within working teams
There is an orderly atmosphere without rigidity	There is an appropriate balance between innovation, tradition, autonomy and authority
There is joint participation in decision making	Teams are recognised as the main focus of effectively maintaining the culture as well as innovating agreed change.

in the school. Their awareness of the need for continuous staff development will, through their skills of administration, go hand in hand with vision, foresight, faith and imagination.

The cultural environment within which these roles exist can be linked to the results-relationship continuum on p 12. At the democratic end the leadership style could be seen as permissive to the extent that teams can operate in isolated 'democratic' groups with little or no strong overall leadership, which is required to make sure that there is a whole school approach. This can allow a fragmented and confused sense of 'who is in charge' but it can also, with consistent, strong and involved leadership, be extremely productive. At the other end of the continuum is autocracy, where decisions tend to be made without any consultation. This can be demoralising in a different way because it denies teachers their professional competence and a chance to develop collective responsibility. Purposeful leadership needs to maintain an environment which fosters the professionalism of teachers and in which the individual teacher can thrive and grow within a team that works to achieve success for everyone. Effective leaders will also want to concentrate on developing the roles of other adults working in school in order to encourage a positive ethos and effective learning culture.

Developing coherence

The culture and atmosphere of any school is greatly influenced by the degree to which it functions as a coherent whole. That is, the extent to which staff have agreed ways of doing things that are consistent, or consistently applied, throughout the school, and which have the support of all staff.

Levels of leadership

When we examine leadership, we have to examine the role of the headteacher but we shouldn't lose sight of the fact that although the headteacher has many responsibilities in terms of leadership, there are others within the school who need similar skills. In many ways leadership is a function of the whole staff team and not just the responsibility of a named individual. Leadership roles can be divided into three broad areas, not all of which may be the sole responsibility of the head:

❑ **Roles relating to other people** – This is where leaders have to act as a kind of figurehead who, for example, speaks at functions such as PTA meetings, open evenings for new parents, curriculum meetings, Christmas concerts, etc. In this role, the leader has also to be able to supervise, select, train and motivate the staff in the school. This is often achieved by liaising with different individuals and different teams and departments, and also includes running or chairing staff meetings, departmental meetings, governors meetings, etc.
❑ **Roles relating to the collection and passing on of information** – This role involves three basic processes: 1) monitoring, fact finding and assessing the needs of the school by department or project, by information gathering from individuals, teams, documents and reports; 2) disseminating information and communicating it to whoever needs it;

3) communicating the school's views to pupils, parents, inspectors, governors, education officers and other stakeholders.

❏ **Roles involving making decisions** – A school cannot function without decisions being made effectively. Chapter 2 looks in more detail at how teams and groups of teachers can work together to make decisions. However, effective decision making may often involve consultation and consensus, meaning that leaders such as headteachers have to find strategies within which to work. Many decisions that involve change will mean balancing the needs of individuals and teams. As this is seen by everyone as a very difficult task, it is important to involve as many colleagues as possible and to be prepared to state quite clearly why certain decisions have been taken. Doing this will involve more than a role in the structure of the school, it will need a leadership style. This is a style of working that will be capable of listening to and embracing conflicting views and being capable of bringing together different beliefs before making any decisions.

LEADERSHIP STYLES

Such opposites as democratic versus autocratic and directive versus permissive are not very helpful because they imply that one is effective and the other isn't. Autocratic leadership, for example, will not achieve certain goals. The move towards collegiality, where the vision is shared and is not exclusive to the headteacher, makes it doubtful whether autocracy would ever be the ideal 'style'. But when decisions have to be taken about health and safety, the administration of lists, birth dates, class groupings, etc, an instant, autocratic decision may well be the ideal 'style'. Hersey and Blanchard (1982) suggest that there is a continuum of leadership styles which is linked to the maturity of colleagues or what they call 'followers'. In their proposed leadership styles there are four types of behaviour, each of which is appropriate to a particular level of maturity. Beginning with immature colleagues and moving towards those who are mature, they suggest the styles shown in Table 1.5. There are similarities between these suggested styles and the results/relationship continuum on p 12 in this chapter.

Whatever leadership style is developed, it must not encourage dependence on top-down decision making nor stifle creativity and innovation, and it certainly must not be afraid of change. In many ways the continuum proposed by Hersey and Blanchard suggests that leaders lean towards either a task-oriented style or one that is people oriented. A task-oriented

Table 1.5 *A continuum of leadership styles*

▲ **Immature**

Telling style (high on task/content and low on relationships/processes)
Selling style (high on task/content high on relationships/processes)
Participating style (low on task/content high on relationship/processes)
Delegating style (low on task content and low on relationships/processes)

▼ **Mature**

---

style will be present when leaders define and structure all the jobs that they and their colleagues have to do in terms of achieving certain goals. It is sometimes described as 'leadership by objectives'. A people-oriented style, on the other hand, will involve the leader relying on trust, mutual support, avoidance of conflict and concern for the idea and feelings of others to achieve the school's goals. Most leaders do not have a total bias towards either style. It is more true to say that to be effective means being able to adopt the style that fits the job in hand.

But what is the job in hand for a leader in a primary school? Let's look at six key elements and then examine each one in more detail:

1. Leaders provide an example.
2. Leaders provide their organisation with a mission.
3. Leaders provide structures.
4. Leaders need to be considerate.
5. Leaders work in particular contexts.
6. Leaders, by the very role they are taking on, need to affect the way decisions are made.

1. Leaders provide an example

Setting an example is a complex process. It is really about modelling the kinds of behaviour and attitudes that you want the school to have. For example, if you want colleagues to talk about teaching and learning and how to raise standards, you must do the same yourself. Indeed, you must not only talk and discuss but also provide a forum for the discussions to take place. Equally, if you don't want individual teachers to moan quietly about their problems but to bring them out in the open, you will have to set an example and allow this to happen and not ridicule or marginalise problems. Depending on the point of view of those working with you, the example you set may be positive or negative. No one is going to be viewed positively all the time, but over a period of time and through a consensus of opinion it is to be hoped that across a whole series of issues and decisions a balanced judgement may be forthcoming. There are a host of personal and professional qualities involved in the concept of 'setting an example'. Energy, trust, delegation, personal organisation, consideration, dealing with differences, handling disputes, sense of humour and temperament all have a part to play.

2. Leaders provide their organisation with a mission

Every successful school has a sense of direction and a feeling of knowing where it is going. This is not just the aims statement which all schools have, although that is important. The mission is about going somewhere and knowing what is going to happen during the journey. Part of this will be the School Development Plan (discussed on p 29), but it will be mainly about how the leaders in the school can make sure that everyone is moving in the same direction, in the same way and with the same sense of urgency and commitment. The school's mission does not mean that there should be a military exactness nor any sense of religious fervour. But it does mean that there is a commonly held vision of how the school should be working that can be used to stimulate every adult who works in the school as well as children, governors and parents.

3. Leaders provide structures

Structures are the basic organisational building blocks of any school. This has already been discussed earlier in this chapter but briefly, they are concerned with such essentials as class organisation, who teaches whom and where, teams and team leaders, planning processes, times of the school day, meeting schedules, timetables, communication networks, etc. Headteachers and all colleagues who act as leaders are involved in making sure that the school functions effectively within the bounds of these organisational structures. They will be involved in:

❑ providing the structures in the first place;
❑ maintaining all the structures that make the school work effectively;
❑ reshaping and changing the structures where and when necessary;
❑ adapting the structures to different circumstances and rapid change.

4. Leaders need to be considerate

The most effective leaders are capable of understanding the views, feelings and attitudes of all those colleagues who work with them. In other words, they are able to empathise. If headteachers as leaders understand and consider each individual by trying to understand their perspectives and by considering each different situation, then they stand a good chance of improving motivation and commitment to the work and life of the school. If we accept that all colleagues are different then the understanding and consideration that we show them has to be different. For example, if someone wants to be involved in decision making and has a great deal to offer then it is neither understanding nor considerate always to tell them what to do. In the same way, if someone sees the world through hierarchical glasses, it would be inconsiderate and counterproductive to ask them to take part in a constant stream of decision-making processes. Leaders also need to be aware of colleagues' individual circumstances. People can be affected by bereavement, illness, family crises and so on. At such times it is not particularly considerate to ask them to take on a major new role or to make significant changes.

5. Leaders work in particular contexts

The context of the school affects the work of all leaders who are sensitive to the problems and issues that different contexts can raise. As leaders affect schools, so schools affect leaders and how they can exercise leadership. Headteachers and other leaders in a small rural school with supportive parents will work within a very different context from the headteacher and leaders who work in a large, deprived inner city school. But it is very important not to fall into the trap of making such issues as non-supportive parents, inadequate buildings or deprived area an excuse for failure. Of course such contexts will influence attainment and will make both raising standards and reaching high standards extremely difficult, but there are other internal contextual factors which will influence how effective and successful you are and which can operate or not in any school. They are:

❑ the way priorities are decided;
❑ the professional relationships among staff;
❑ the resources available in school;
❑ the level of staff development;
❑ the effectiveness of the headteacher;
❑ the level of support from the LEA.

Because context affects how effective the school can be and because that context can change, from time to time leaders need to assess how their present context is affecting their work, as well as how they, their colleagues and how they work together are affecting the context.

6. Leaders, by the very role they are taking on, need to affect how decisions are taken

There are basically two decision-making processes, known as centralised and decentralised. Centralised means that the headteacher takes on an authoritarian style and all decisions are taken centrally after some discussion with individuals who may have a stake in the decision. Decentralised decisions, however, rely on groups being involved in the process and a dialogue with the headteacher before decisions are taken based on reasoned discussion and shared views involving other people. It could be the case that the authoritarian style actually increases low expectation in teachers who are not expected to have views on decisions that will affect them. If the decision-making process puts teachers into this position, they are very unlikely to show initiative or manage any imposed changes that come their way. They may feel that whatever decisions have been taken are not their responsibility. This in itself may mean that leaders who operate in a centralised, autocratic way and who consistently avoid involving others in planning and decision making are, in fact, whether they realise it or not, teaching their staff to feel incompetent in the processes that lead to decisions and change.

Let us assume that in managing the organisation of the school the following are true:

❑ The ethos and aims of the school are clear and the school's mission or aims statement stands up as the leading principle of how the school intends to move effectively forward.
❑ There are structures in place that will translate the mission statement and the aims and objectives of the school into the kind of reality that will provide an effective and well-taught curriculum. In practice, remember, this will be achieved by delegating responsibilities to deputies and coordinators.
❑ There are leaders and senior professionals in the school with responsibility for managing and motivating both teachers and non-teachers. This epitomises the main role of any headteacher and senior manager, and is about relationships within the school and how to make sure that they are secure and established on the kind of professional trust that means the school will work effectively.

❏   The leadership of the school is able to direct and control how the school is organised, using a structure that is more collegial than autocratic and which is able to take in the views of all interested parties, including teachers, non-teachers, children, parents and governors.

So, all this is in place and the school moves effectively along, but how are all these successes communicated to participants and, even more importantly, how are all these successes developed in the first place if there are not effective methods of communication in place?

COMMUNICATION

Communication is about the sharing of information, attitudes and beliefs and also about the passing on of knowledge and information. No school can be effective unless communication is managed effectively, and this does not just mean that the headteacher or the deputy headteacher is an effective communicator. This will be no help at all if no one is receiving the message.

Communication has to be appropriate to its purpose, the situation in which it is taking place, and the audience and readership for whom it is intended. In a successful school this will mean that information for colleagues will move upwards, sideways and downwards and that there will be feedback to check that information has been received and that communication has been successful.

A simple reason for making sure that information is shared is to ensure that jobs get done and that the right messages reach the right people at the right time. This kind of essential information in schools can be separated into three types: long-term, medium-term and short-term communication. This is shown in Table 1.6.

Successful communication in a school will make sure that the organisation functions efficiently. Poor communication, on the other hand, will lead to frustration because essential messages, whether long, medium or short term, do not reach those who need them. Any effective manager will have set up routes within his or her organisation to pass the information on to those who need to receive it. Unfortunately, no matter how efficient the structures of communication, such as notice boards, diaries and memos, they will all fail to work if colleagues misinterpret or block messages. Methods of preventing communication, or erecting barriers to slow down, alter and divert messages or information, include:

Table 1.6 *Three types of communication*

Long-term communication consists mainly of those documents that are the umbrella under which the school works. They are such things as subject policies, behaviour, marking, anti-bullying and SEN policies and the School Development Plan. They need to be shared among all staff so that no one needs to work alone with their own agendas and everyone has a coherent view of the school's aims, beliefs and ways of working.

Medium-term communications are those which refine the long-term issues into working documents. In translating long-term issues into action plans there will be schemes of work for each subject and for each block of time, such as a half or full term. The School Development Plan, for example, will need to be broken down into manageable sections, with a specific person being responsible for finishing the task by way of medium-term action plans that have a completion date.

Short-term communication is concerned with the day-to-day messages that have to be given to individuals and groups because otherwise the structure of each day and each week would be chaotic.

❏ censoring what has been communicated by only recognising what is welcome and discarding what is not;
❏ having an emotional interest in the information and allowing this to get in the way of the real message;
❏ distrusting the information by not believing anything passed on by certain colleagues;
❏ distorting the message by passing on information that is only a partial reflection of the original;
❏ being confused by too much information and not knowing what to do with it;
❏ being in conflict with colleagues and withholding information;
❏ keeping information secret.

All these negative factors, which inhibit and neutralise important information, need to be removed, because good communications within a school imply a well-designed and healthy organisation. It is not unreasonable to suggest, therefore, that it is important to manage internal communication within a structured plan. Communication in a school is often inferred, in that colleagues and visitors will make inferences from each other's dress, manner, tone of voice, etc.

Of course different people will infer different things. A headteacher might assume that just because s/he has an open door policy and doesn't hide behind a desk, colleagues will find it easy to talk and discuss relevant issues. Teachers, however, might disagree and suggest that despite the open door s/he is still a difficult person to talk to. This may also be true of the physical environment. Certain messages will be sent to visitors and colleagues in the form of closed doors, formal seating arrangements, and even such notices as 'no entry' or 'do not knock' etc.

To prevent the kinds of problems related to what happens when people make different interpretations of what is communicated in school, there has to be a formal system of communication which, through meetings, papers, documents and policies, enables everything that needs to be known to be relayed accurately to everyone who needs the information.

The range of material is vast, and without careful planning the amount can be overwhelming. It needs to be broken down into manageable chunks. One of the obvious ways of doing this is to make sure that these 'chunks' are important enough for people to understand and that they are sent by the simplest and most direct method. This is not easy, because some long-term issues may involve meetings over a period of time whereas others will be no more than a short conversation in a corridor. Obviously, the larger the school, the more complex the organisation and the more difficult it is to monitor how effective communication is. The small school, however, where everyone works closely together, often has problems when everyone assumes, sometimes wrongly, that all teachers know about everything that is going on. Whatever the size of the organisation, however, it is useful to recognise that if change is to be handled effectively, if standards are to be raised and if collegiality is to be an accepted way of working, it is necessary to accept Southworths' (1990) suggestion of the importance of interaction, communication and in-school dialogue concerning teaching and learning styles and curriculum content. It is also important to recognise that a school with a closed system of communication, where no one is told anything that they don't need to know, will not operate as successfully or as effectively as a school where everyone is kept informed of everything that isn't private and confidential. This kind of open system will also reduce suspicion and enable staff to be more willing to develop and sustain a communication network where everyone is responsible for sharing information.

Face-to-face communication

Teachers need to be encouraged to talk to each other about what they are doing. In fact, the more the organisation is geared to discussions about teaching and learning and the more knowledge that is shared, the more effective the school is likely to be. Talking to colleagues is a kind of collaboration between teachers where they discuss and disseminate the community knowledge of the school.

Headteachers talk to teachers both formally and informally, and in the medium and long term there are meetings where face-to-face interaction is how ideas are communicated. The main characteristic of this kind of communication is the ability to listen, and those who are least likely to listen are more likely to mishear or not hear at all and consequently to make more mistakes. Some of the rules for listening are as follows:

❏ Allow the person who is talking to finish speaking, and avoid completing sentences or making it obvious that you are burning to say something.
❏ Try not to think about the next point or you will miss what is being said.
❏ Use your memory to recognise key points. It is often an aid to everyone's memory if you begin your reply by restating the key points that have been made.
❏ Be objective rather than subjective and try not to let your interpretation of what is being said be distorted by any adverse feelings you have about the speaker's clothes, appearance or manner.

Another aspect of making sure that face-to-face encounters are effective is the ability to recognise several interactive styles which will improve the method of sharing information. These styles will include:

❏ Colleagues who are friendly and who smile, nod, have a relaxed posture and maintain eye contact.
❏ Those who will want to dominate and control. They might point at colleagues, lean forward when speaking, interrupt, ignore responses and use a controlling tone of voice.
❏ Unfortunately, there are some colleagues who are both unresponsive and aggressive. They will stare, have a set mouth and face, keep an inappropriate distance, speak in a harsh tone of voice and have abrupt movement and speech.

❏ Some colleagues will be timid and submissive. They will be nervous, avoid eye contact, allow colleagues to interrupt them and speak hesitantly in a soft tone of voice.

Much of the communication that takes place in school is fragmentary and on its own is relatively insignificant. Taken together, there will be a consolidation of shared ideas and a belief in the effectiveness of sharing information that will help raise standards. At the same time, there is essential information that has to be shared with teachers and those outside the immediate professional circle, such as parents and governors. Doing this successfully will make sure that the school as an organisation is seen both in a positive light and as effective in what it is trying to do. This information will include the School Development Plan or School Improvement Plan, information on individual children as written reports or face-to-face discussions during parents' evenings, the governors' annual report to parents, and the school prospectus.

Methods of communication between the school, parents and governors

Effective communication between home and school is important, and failing to build up a strong partnership with parents will disadvantage both pupils and teachers. In fact, schools need to see themselves in partnership with everyone who has a vested interest in the school. To achieve a level of collegiality and teamwork that supports this partnership, as much information as possible needs to pass backwards and forwards between school and home and school and governors. Governors need all the information that is necessary for them to be able to take strategic decisions about the school. Brehony (1992) uses the term 'active citizenship' to describe part of the governors' role. It is also suggested that the relationship between schools and governors should be one of democracy and accountability, and that both concepts need clear communication if they are to be effective.

Schools with a positive ethos and a clear idea that they want and need to share all kinds of information with parents will send regular 'newsletters', both as whole school letters from the headteacher and as specific information from individual teachers about such diverse issues as what their class or year group are being taught, how parents can help and information about visits out of school. There also needs to be available in school all the policy documents that are relevant for parents to read. For example, parents will be interested in those on anti-bullying, behaviour and homework. It is also important to sell the school to existing and potential parents as a vibrant, open institution. This will mean arranging formal and informal visits to the school, including open days where parents can see what the school is like during a working day. There should also be an input into the life of the effective school by parents through a thriving parent–teacher organisation, with social events such as dances, quizzes and wine-tasting evenings. Parent governors should also want to communicate with parents both as part of their statutory duties and to increase the effectiveness of home–school liaison. If a school has had a recent OFSTED inspection, a summary of the report has to be sent to all parents together with a summary of the post-OFSTED action plans.

Much of this communication is concerned with 'accountability' and letting the world see how the school is functioning effectively. Many of the methods of external communication will be similar to those occurring within the school, and will demand the familiar skills related to meetings, face-to-face communication and written documents. What is important, however, is that these skills need to be matched to the specific audience that is being targeted. For example, written communication to parents should represent long-term information such as the year's calendar, but it should also have short-term messages about current issues and current events. Many of the methods of communication will depend on what the school wants to do and what it is prepared to do. Several areas, however, are subject to legislation, such as the governor's annual reports to parents, school test results together with comparisons with national results and children's annual written reports.

Open evenings/parent evenings

Mortimore *et al* (1988) see parental involvement in the life of the school as a positive influence on pupils' progress and development, and recognise how important it is for parents to attend. Throughout the year there will be many informal opportunities to meet parents, but at set times, and this should ideally be every term, there will be pre-arranged open evenings with individual appointments for parents to discuss the progress of their child. These meetings are a golden opportunity to communicate and share concerns and for teachers to sell the school and their own professional skills by conveying to parents a strong sense of their personal interest in each pupil.

Governors' annual report to parents

This report and the subsequent meeting with parents are related directly to accountability. This is the main opportunity for governors to justify to parents the issues that they have considered and the decisions they have taken during the previous year. Unfortunately, this task and any discussion and feedback from parents are hampered by the notoriously low turnout at the annual meeting, and although this might suggest that such meetings should be avoided, there is in fact a statutory obligation. Like the meeting itself, much of the content of the report is statutory. It includes such areas as a budget summary, Special Educational Needs, attendance figures, report on items considered from the previous year's meeting, reports from governor's subcommittees, and test results, including a comparison of the school's results with national test results. Many headteachers, teachers, governors and, I would suspect, many parents consider that performance indicators such as test results and rates of what is, in effect, truancy in the form of unauthorised absences do not, when presented as lists of figures and percentages, reflect the true worth and true popularity and effectiveness of an individual school. By giving them separate and by definition higher status, there is the danger that they are given a false sense of importance in defining school success and school effectiveness.

School prospectus

A well-structured, colourful, carefully edited and well-printed prospectus is an ideal way to sell your school to as wide an audience as possible. It should be the kind of publicity material that reflects the quality of service that the school is able to offer. In selling the school's image, its contents need to reflect the kind of corporate image that teachers, governors and parents want. In fact, they should be involved in taking decisions about the content and in the production and design. Different schools will want to communicate different information, but there are huge areas of the brochure where legislation dictates what has to be included. As well as prescribing much of the content, there is also legislation stating that it needs to be available to anyone who is interested and that it must be free. The content has changed frequently and there is no reason to think that there will not be more changes in the future. Table 1.7 summarises the most recent content.

In deciding on what to write in those sections related to 'school ethos and values', such areas as school discipline, extra curricular activities, school aims statement, etc, might have to be included.

Table 1.7 *Content of the governors' annual report to parents*

Admission arrangements

Assessment results and comparisons with national test results (as a loose leaf if the prospectus will last for more than one year)

The number of places available, ie the school's standard number for the purposes of admission (if there is the possibility of over-subscription and subsequent waiting lists the number of applications in the previous year has to be stated)

Practical detains such as address, telephone number, names of headteacher and chair of governors

Calendar of the year's events (on a loose leaf if much of the prospectus is going to last for more than one year)

Summary of charges and admissions policy

Rates of unauthorised absences

Details of arrangements made for SEN pupils and those with statements of SEN

Summary of content and organisation of the school's sex education policy

Details of RE and collective worship

Statements on the curriculum organisation and teaching methods

Statement on the ethos and values of the school

Once again, the school's prospectus, as well as being a marketing tool, is a public document that is a further part of the school's process of accountability. Effective schools will take a proactive stance and make sure that the prospectus has an impact on parental support.

School Development Plan or School Improvement Plan

This is at the core of an effective school. It is the plan that states what is going to be done within the next two to three years; it should say clearly who 'owns' each section of the plan; when each stage is going to be completed; how progress is going to be reported back to governors, staff and parents; and how everyone will know when each section has been successfully completed. It will also need to identify training and staff development needs and areas where, in order to succeed, money will need to be made available. All schools have to have a Development or Improvement Plan, and many schools see the plan as an effective tool for raising standards. Ideally, such a plan should be devised by staff, parents and governors. This will make sure that advantage has been takes of a wide range of expertise and knowledge. However, the more people involved, the greater the possible tensions and the slower the process, but the end product will be 'owned' by all the participants. According to the DfEE *Development Planning: A Practical Guide* (1995), the School Development Plan 'is a plan of needs for development set in the context of the school's aims and values, its existing achievements and national and LEA policies and initiatives. Detailed objectives are set for one year, the objectives for later years are sketched in outline' (1991: 2). It seems to me that it is unreasonable to expect to organise any school so that it has a positive ethos simply by expecting it to happen because of purely random events. There has to be detailed senior management and whole school planning. Changes are happening so fast and are so urgent that they must be managed in a professional way. If random elements are allowed to be the main method of planning and decision making, then they will inevitably become the norm and everyone involved with the school will be so overloaded and confused by an unplanned mass of competing priorities that nothing of value will emerge and nothing that has been written in the plan will be sustained. Writing, structuring and creating the School Development Plan can be made easier if it is based on the following structure, which provides a clear and practical way forward:

❏ Evidence that identifies the school's needs and the school's strengths and weaknesses needs to be collected from as wide a range of sources as possible.
❏ Priorities need to be established from such a bank of evidence. This will mean that a list is made of what has been identified as needing to be done in order to move the school forward and to raise standards.
❏ These priorities have to be broken down into manageable actions, and these actions need to have a person who is responsible for them and a time limit for completion.
❏ The time element needs to be practical and manageable. It is important, in a three-year plan, that everything that has been identified is not prioritised in such a way that it has a completion date in the first year of the plan.
❏ In writing the plan for each year, with the first year containing detailed actions and an outline for subsequent years, the following points must be considered:
   – What is the action that needs to be taken ?
   – Who is involved (this needs to be an individual who is responsible for the action being completed and perhaps a team of colleagues to plan the action)?

- Are there budget and training implications?
- What are the expected outcomes?
- How will the plan be monitored and evaluated in terms of its successes?

It is impossible to suggest a list of priorities because schools will have different areas of need. Most schools will, however, have some aspects of raising standards in literacy and numeracy within their School Development Plan. There should also be sections on school management, the school site, and perhaps how information is shared between different stakeholders in the school, ie communication. A successful plan has to work in practice and has to have involved a wide cross-section of the school community. If this happens, the whole process will help teachers, for example by increasing their confidence that they have some control over what is happening and by improving the quality of staff development. After all, if you are saying that certain things must happen, there need to be training opportunities to make sure that what you say is going to happen actually does. If the head-teacher and perhaps one senior colleague complete the plan and present it to staff and governors as the School Development Plan, it is unlikely that such a plan will work. It may well be that at the end of the plan, although there should be frequent monitoring, very little will have been achieved. Each teacher needs to play a part and each governor needs to have had the opportunity of being consulted. By doing this there will be an ethos of working together to achieve the aims of the school, which is the subject of Chapter 2.

The pupil's annual report

There has to be at least an annual written report. Some schools may feel that reports should be written more frequently. Certainly for children with statements of Special Educational Needs there are at least termly reviews that do have a written element. The 'report' on an individual child should ideally be about positive progress and expectations for the future. At one level, however, parents and teachers will expect the report to be wide ranging and to cover many topics, including the progress of the pupil; at another level, the parent will be a consumer and will expect the school to report precise outcomes and to be held accountable for the test results and progress of their child. There are certain details that have to be included in an annual report to parents and, in the case of primary schools, many important details such as social and personal comments are missing from the legislation. Schools will have to balance the requirements of what most parents want and what is required by the various Education Acts. Report writing by hand is time consuming, but there are several computer programs available with large comment banks for teachers to use. These can be invaluable in that they include far more information about the National Curriculum than can be remembered or hand written. Most programs can also be changed to meet the needs of individual schools. As with the requirements of the content of the prospectus, the list that closes this chapter is the current legislation. This does not mean that it cannot or will not change radically in the future. The areas that have to be written into the report to parents include:

❑ comments on all National Curriculum subjects covered;
❑ comments on general progress in all subjects and activities not mentioned elsewhere, including such areas as cross-curricular work, PSHE, social and personal progress;
❑ succinct comments covering a pupil's individual progress, including strengths, weaknesses and achievements;
❑ test results where applicable, ie at age 7 (Y2) and age 11 (Y6);
❑ comparative information about attainment of all pupils of the same age (Years 2 and 6);
❑ comparative information about attainments of the same age groups nationally;
❑ attendance record.

IMPORTANT POINTS

❑ How the school is organised will have a profound impact on whether its ethos and culture are recognised as effective, successful and positive by pupils, teachers, parents and governors.
❑ The basic organisation has to be effective. This will include an aims statement that sets the whole tone of what happens in school, who does what in terms of responsibilities, class organisation, the kind of leadership and who holds power in the school.
❑ There are different kinds of organisation that will apply to different types of school and this will depend on such things as the size of the school, its design, whether it is managed hierarchically or collegially.
❑ Leadership is a key factor in school effectiveness. This begins with the headteacher but will also include how subject coordinators are organised and how much leadership they are allowed and expected to use.
❑ Communication is at the heart of how effective the organisation of the school is. This means not only the kind of face-to-face discussions about teaching and learning that take place, but also the key documents that hold the school accountable and 'sell' it to parents and governors.

RELATIONSHIPS IN THE SCHOOL

This chapter looks at:

- how teams are built and how they work together;
- leading the team;
- the effective team;
- how decisions are managed;
- methods of decision making;
- how groups and teams are successful;
- resolving conflict;
- assertiveness;
- the positive colleague.

It considers the importance of relationships between adults and how they work together to take decisions and the ways in which school leaders can improve this process.

INTRODUCTION

Positive working relationships will not develop unless there is trust and for me to suggest a working atmosphere where trust is the norm we will have to return to the concept of the collegial school which was introduced in Chapter 1.

Collegial schools

Collegial schools have to work in the following ways:

- There is a general and widespread agreement on the aims and purposes of the school.

❏ Decision making that affects what happens in the school is seen as a corporate event which involves colleagues.
❏ Individual teachers are recognised as experts in different areas and this expertise is valued and used.
❏ Discussions and decision making take place without acrimony or alienation.
❏ The ethos and culture of the school support colleagues working together to develop professional and social cohesion and collaboration.

All of these areas are linked to the kinds of relationships that have to be established and maintained. The more people who work together to make decisions, the more they will feel involved and be committed to making decisions work. Teachers will also feel that they know what is happening. They will have been consulted and will not only have a wide spread of influence but there will be more opportunities for individual teachers to develop their own skills without feeling isolated. Rather than diminish the leadership of the headteacher, a collegial approach will enhance it and enrich his or her role because of the wide-ranging contributions of other colleagues. Collegiality is useful because it demonstrates that professionals can and should work together for the benefit of the team. If this happens in a school it will have a positive effect on teaching and learning.

Working relationships

But, like all the issues discussed in this chapter and in the whole book, successful relationships within the school organisation don't just happen. In fact it takes more than planning, organisation and action to create this kind of effective way for colleagues to work together. It requires a knowledge of and an allowance for the way people feel. The attitudes of teachers to each other and to the senior teachers and headteacher and the attitudes of the headteacher to everyone who works in the school are vital to the success of how the school is organised and how relationships help in the move towards raising standards.

We are arguing that collegiality and not relying totally on a hierarchical top-down decision-making process is going to be more effective than any other style of management. Let's stop for a moment and stress that this does not mean that there is no strong leadership or accountability to senior management nor that headteachers do not make judgements about the quality of teaching and learning. It does mean, however, that more people share in the process of decision making, sharing ideas and making judgements on how effective the school is and what needs to happen to make it even more successful. The success of how colleagues work together will depend largely on the interpersonal relationships that are formed. These in turn will largely be determined by how the headteacher and teaching staff take into account personal individual factors when working together for the good of the school.

Some of the more common characteristics are listed in Table 2.1 The table should not contain any surprises and yet it is surprising how many colleagues that you work with will not have the interpersonal skills to take full advantage of working together within groups of people who share these sophisticated qualities.

Table 2.1 *Characteristics that determine good working relationships*

Approachability of all staff to other colleagues, children, parents, etc.
Appreciation of other people's points of view
Understanding and concern for the welfare of colleagues
Sympathy towards the views of colleagues
The ability to inspire trust in colleagues
Tolerance of other people's ideas
A sense of humour
The ability to share problems and help solve them
The willingness to praise and to accept praise
The ability to listen and to be tolerant
Being able to face up to conflict and work to reduce and remove the source of the conflict
Knowing when to set tight deadlines and when to minimise any pressure on colleagues.
The ability to be fair and just and to be seen as fair and just
Knowing when to be just part of a working team and when to lead, cajole, persuade and pressurise
The ability to continue to be enthusiastic despite any conflict and problems

HOW TEAMS ARE BUILT AND HOW THEY WORK TOGETHER

High quality interpersonal relationships are a start to good relationships within schools, but to work as an effective whole school team or in smaller

̶ ̶ ̶making teams means developing a high level of collaboration and an ability to work towards consensus. Neither is easy and there are four issues that need to be considered.

1. To collaborate and achieve consensus takes time

Putting teachers together and hoping and assuming that they will 'get on with' whatever job they are doing or decision that they are taking doesn't work. First, there needs to be an assumption that collaboration and consensus are the norm. But working together in teams is not easy and will not happen without some careful thought and hard work. Handy (1976) shows that groups take time and effort to develop into teams that will work effectively together. He suggests that they 'mature and develop. Like individuals they have a fairly clearly defined growth cycle' (1976: 160).

Table 2.2 summarises Handy's four stages of how groups will build into effective teams. It is important that this happens over as short a period of time as possible because the whole point of teams working collaboratively together is that they are more likely to produce better solutions than an individual on his or her own.

These stages are relatively common and it needs to be recognised that it is not easy to reach stage 4 where the team 'performs'. Problems will continue to arise with group members who fail to contribute, who continue to see no meaning in the task and whose personalities are such that they clash with other team members. Some of these issues will be raised later in the chapter.

2. Effective teamwork is essential for collaboration to be successful

Teams working together have to be productive; they have to get the work done successfully and on time. On some occasions individual team members might hinder this process, and this is important enough to be discussed in more detail later in the chapter. In general terms, however, one way of finding out whether the teams in your school are as effective as they should be is to ask some key questions such as:

❑   Do our meetings go on too long?
❑   Are the number of meetings and/or the pattern of meetings appropriate for the job that has to be done?

36

Table 2.2 *Groups into effective teams*

---

1. The group *forms*
Most groups form around one person who is the leader because there is a problem to be solved in that changes need to be made and decisions need to be taken. At this stage most group members are anxious and over-dependent on the leader. This is a time of testing the water, as no one is quite sure what behaviour is acceptable to other group members who will all be finding out what the task is, how they are going to go about it and what the expected outcome will be.

2. The group *storms*
This second stage is common to most groups. It occurs when members do not get on and there is conflict between sub-groups and often rebellion against the leader. It is difficult to suggest why this happens. There will certainly be resistance to 'control', and it is as if group members have to assert their individuality rather than merge into the whole group. There is also resistance to actually getting on with the job in hand and most group members will feel that the task has no particular interest for them.

3. The group *norms*
During this stage, the group begins to work together as a team and a more collaborative pattern of behaviour appears. This happens because resistance to the leader or to the task has been overcome and conflicts are resolved and there is a mutual feeling of support. It is at this stage that a lot of the work gets done because there is an open exchange of views and greater cooperation in trying to reach sensible and valuable decisions.

4. The group *performs*
The group is now a working team moving towards solving problems and achieving outcomes. They want to finish the job. There are few interpersonal problems and team members know each other well and have developed a working relationship that allows them to move forward. Solutions and outcomes emerge and there will be constructive attempts to meet any deadlines that have been set.

❑ Have we got the right people and the right number of people in the group?
❑ How can we make the team meetings more effective?

Table 2.3 *Establishing the effectiveness of a team*

1. *Aims of the team*
POOR   GOOD
Conflicting, unclear,   1 2 3 4 5   Clear to everyone, shared,
 having little interest   everyone feels involved

2. *Taking part*
POOR   GOOD
A few colleagues   1 2 3 4 5   Everyone is listened to, no
dominate. Some   one dominates and all
colleagues are passive,   views count
some are not listened to.
Several talk at once and
interrupt

3. *How do team members feel?*
POOR   GOOD
Ignored, not listened to,   1 2 3 4 5   Part of the team, listened
criticised, ridiculed   to, happy to work in the
                                              team

4. *Leadership of the group*
POOR   GOOD
No one takes control as   1 2 3 4 5   One leader is willing and
'chair'. Everyone relies   able to control the team.
too much on a single   Everyone feels free to take
person. No one   over leadership when
summarises or takes any   necessary
notes or minutes

5. *Team decisions*
POOR   GOOD
Decisions don't get taken,   1 2 3 4 5   Consensus is wanted and
or decisions are made by   disagreements are used to
part of the group without   improve decisions.
proper agreement or   Decisions taken are fully
consensus   supported

6. *Trusting colleagues in the team*
POOR   GOOD
Team members distrust   1 2 3 4 5   Team members trust each
each other. They listen and   other. They respect each

talk superficially and then reject proposals. Team members are afraid to criticise and to be criticised

other's responses and can express contrary views freely

7. Ability to take decisions that would make changes
POOR   GOOD

Team members are in a rut and can only operate routinely, without any creativity. Individuals are stereotyped in their roles and are unable to make any progress

1 2 3 4 5

The team is flexible and seeks new and better ways to make changes. Individual members of the team are changing and growing

Answers to these general questions will help you reach conclusions about some of the reasons why teams in your school are effective or less so, as the case may be. Table 2.3 is a more precise and systematic way of finding out about your teams. It can be used each time a team completes a task over a period of time or used each term to consider the effectiveness of a series of meetings. To complete the table, put a ring round the appropriate number on the five-point scale.

3. If there are differences they need to be faced

Differences of opinion can mean conflict and if there is conflict and it is not resolved quickly, time will be wasted and jobs will not be completed (there is a section on conflict resolution later in the chapter). Both collaboration and consensus can lead to conflict and it is important that differences are worked through rather than left to simmer and continue to prevent problems being solved. While this is not always comfortable, it is necessary. If conflict is not resolved it will go underground and create more long-term difficulties. Conflict is often about negative feelings and not necessarily about what is being discussed and the kinds of changes that are being planned. One way of avoiding this negativity is to make sure that the social and informal aspects of school life are well maintained. For example, are the team meetings at the right time and in the right place? Is the furniture appropriate for the task in hand? Are there coffee- and tea-making facilities? It is also the case that groups of colleagues who are able to talk to each other about their personal and social lives are more likely to discuss professional issues as a working and effective team.

4. Consensus does not always mean that consent has been given

Let's first make some assumptions about issues that have already been discussed. All your colleagues are able to work within a team that has 'formed' and is 'performing'. They are a cohesive group who are well led and they are able to share and air their differences in a creative way. They work in their teams within a school where there is a culture of discussion about education, teaching and learning and where collaboration between colleagues is the norm. Even with all these optimum conditions it is not always possible to achieve consensus, because consensus means that there is full agreement and that decisions are close to being unanimous. This is difficult, if not impossible, to achieve because when professional colleagues meet together there are bound to be different personal and professional opinions and different views on a range of educational and non-educational issues. To achieve consensus in most circumstances in school and within reasonable time limits is not realistically achievable. What is possible, however, and what should be accepted in any working team, is 'consent' or the ability to be able to accept a proposal and give it as good a try as possible. Schools should shy away from the neurosis that sometimes goes by the name of 'striving for excellence' and think more in terms of being as 'good as possible in the present circumstance'. Working towards consensus is fine but accepting consent is realistic and achievable.

LEADING THE TEAM

An effective headteacher will always try to operate with a spirit of participation, trust, negotiation and responsibility. This should also be the philosophy of every senior manager or subject coordinator who is leading a planning or decision-making team. Leadership in this context does not just apply to the headteacher. The more the 'leader' consults by presenting a problem, getting suggestions and working towards a decision, and the more they share by asking for consensus and/or consent, the more professional colleagues will feel a sense of freedom, participation and investment in a solution. Some of the skills needed to work in this way are listed in Table 2.4. Many of these skills have been at the edge of earlier discussions and

Table 2.4 *Team leadership skills*

Summarising skills
Negotiating skills
Open-ended questioning skills
Selecting the key points in arguments
Focussing on key issues
Evaluating the strength of different points of view
Timing skills in knowing when to move on and when to stop
Listening skills
Non-verbal skills to identify team member's attitudes and feelings

---

they will all depend on a leader who possesses a variety of skills that will help them to lead effective discussions.

It is important that the team leader is able to demonstrate that they have the ability to negotiate sympathetically; listen, take notes and take decisions; make sure that individual needs are accounted for; ensure that there is continuity and support; and that after every team meeting, colleagues leave the discussion with a sense of achievement.

THE EFFECTIVE TEAM

There is sometimes a clash between the needs of the individual and the needs of the team. This is mainly because individuals like to feel a responsibility for implementing and sharing in the development of change without really sacrificing their individuality. They like to have responsibility and to be trusted and they also need to see a benefit to themselves and to the school. Whoever is leading the team needs to be good at negotiation and able to contribute to an individual's autonomy as well as seeing through the task that the team has been set.

It is also true to say that the changes that the team are working on need to be prioritised. It may be better to leave some tasks until later and concentrate on those that are seen as the most important. Doing this is not easy and will depend on setting clear and achievable objectives that will:

❑   be mutually agreeable;
❑   specify what has to be accomplished;

Table 2.5 *How do you know that your team is effective?*

An effective team:
1. shares objectives and goals and has clear procedures:
   - ❏ agrees on priorities;
   - ❏ clarifies the roles of the team members;
   - ❏ has clear procedures for organising meetings, making decisions and delegating responsibilities;

2. reviews its procedures regularly:
   - ❏ reassesses its objectives;
   - ❏ evaluates the processes the team is using;
   - ❏ doesn't spend too much time reassessing the past and what has already been decided;

3. has leadership appropriate to its membership:
   - ❏ has a leader who is visible and accessible;
   - ❏ has a leader who is capable of utilising the strengths of all the team members;

4. has open lines of communication:
   - ❏ has team members who talk to each other about issues that they are dealing with;
   - ❏ has team members who recognise and accept contributions by colleagues;
   - ❏ gives positive and negative feedback;
   - ❏ consists of colleagues who are open to other people's arguments;
   - ❏ welcomes advice from outside sources;

5. has a climate of support and trust:
   - ❏ gives and receives support from colleagues;
   - ❏ has team members who spend enough time together to function effectively;
   - ❏ identifies and builds on team members' strengths;
   - ❏ respects other people's views.

❏ set a target date for its accomplishment;
❏ be realistic.

If the effective team is able to set objectives in terms of priorities and to 'perform' in such a way that results are achieved, it should be possible to suggest ways of recognising the team's ability to achieve. In other words, how do you know when a team of colleagues is effective? Table 2.5 is a checklist of the characteristics of an effective team. It applies to all teams, from those that consist of senior teachers or senior managers to those that are formed to solve a short-term curriculum issue.

HOW DECISIONS ARE MANAGED

Whether we are setting targets, objectives or goals, managing important changes or just coping with the details of day-to-day organisation, we have to make things happen in the way we want them to happen. Our success or failure will largely depend on our ability to take and implement decisions. A considerable amount of emphasis has been placed on working together, and it is certainly the case that teams and groups can, should and do take decisions. However, leadership, and don't forget that groups and teams have leaders, will mean that one person will take the final decision and be held accountable for the decision that has been taken.

Taking decisions

Decisions mean that something has to happen. You don't usually take decisions that say nothing will change and everything will stay the same. So decision making will often be a difficult process involving change, conflict and the risk of being wrong. This, of course, will mean that many people would rather do anything than take the final decision that commits colleagues to a certain course of action. If this happens in your school there will be problems, because failing to take a decision can be worse by making colleagues start to feel frustrated and almost paralysed by a lack of decision. In many surveys which ask employees what they want their boss to do more frequently, the answer almost always centres around decision making, that is, he or she should take decisions . . . and, it is often said, take them more clearly or more rapidly. If, however, there is a blame culture in your school, decision making may be slow, ponderous and occur less often than it should. There needs to be a culture of problem solving, but not of blame, because the risk of not deciding is often the greatest of all risks to the organisation's efficiency and effectiveness. Whether the decision is taken by an individual or in the context of a team of colleagues, there is a series of logical steps which are illustrated in Table 2.6. These steps are important (descriptions of them follow), because it is all too easy to go straight for the 'easy' first solution that is suggested without considering the side effects

Table 2.6 *Step-by-step decision making*

1. Define the situation.
2. Establish criteria.
3. Generate alternatives.
4. Evaluate and test.
5. Select.

that might be generated and the possible alternatives which might be better for both the organisation of the school and the relationships within it.

Step 1 Defining the situation

This should take place within a team that is working on a particular project, although even in this situation it may well be the headteacher who sifts through the reported evidence and takes the final decision. Let's imagine a situation in which a team of teachers is working on improving Open Evenings because parents are complaining that they have to wait around too much. It is useful to look at the issues in the following ways:

❏ What is the situation at the moment?
❏ What should the situation be?
❏ Where does the problem occur most often?
❏ What is the 'ideal' that we should like to see?

Often it is useful to restate the problem in as many ways as possible. The more specific we can be, the better. After trying to define the situation, the original issue that parents are complaining of, namely having to wait around too much, might change to '10 parents out of 150 have complained, or 'some parents in certain areas of the school are bored waiting for appointments'. This will entail a very different solution, such as not changing the structure of Open Evenings at all, but putting up more interesting displays, providing refreshments or having different computer programs available.

Step 2 What needs to happen

When the problem has been identified, it is useful to think in terms of what is essential in order to achieve what you want to achieve and what is desirable. An example we could use is that of children having their snacks stolen from their lunch boxes. The criteria for a satisfactory solution would be:

❏ Essential: thefts from lunch boxes will not occur and parents will no longer have anything to complain about.
❏ Desirable: children should not have to check their lunch boxes to see if everything is still there; children should be able to leave their lunch boxes in the appropriate place; would-be thieves will be deterred.

Step 3 Generate alternative courses of action

The fact that the headteacher or a group of colleagues have to build up the kind of relationships that allows them to take a decision implies that there is more than one course of action. There are often several alternatives and this is what can make decision making so difficult. The task of finding the right alternative can call for a high degree of discussion, sharing of ideas, and clear and effective thinking. Two useful approaches are: 1) inviting colleagues to share in the decision making, which will happen frequently when teams are working on solving a particular problem; and 2) using a space of time to think about the problem, which can be described as 'sleeping on' it and can be very useful, providing the procrastination doesn't last too long.

Step 4 Evaluating and testing alternative courses of action

What you are really doing here is comparing the alternatives generated in Step 3 with the criteria from Step 2. Any alternatives that don't satisfy the 'essential' criteria can be weeded out immediately. In our 'stealing from lunch boxes' example, we could immediately rule out such feeble alternatives as doing nothing, or having a quiet word in assembly. Some alternatives that might work and have the desirable effect include: carrying out an investigation to try to identify the thief; setting a trap; establishing a group of children to watch the lunch boxes; providing a secure area for the lunch boxes. Each of these alternatives might move some way towards satisfying the 'essential' and the 'desirable' criteria.

Step 5 Selecting the right course of action

Most alternatives will have disadvantages. The choice that has to be made will have to be a balanced judgement in which we are aware of all the potential snags and in which we weigh the relative priorities. Whatever the decision, it has to be both made and implemented wholeheartedly.

METHODS OF DECISION MAKING

Teamwork is an excellent way of getting things done and deciding the kind of decision that needs taking. It is true that quite often the relationships within the team can be fragile and occasionally fracture, but consensus and agreement can make better decisions. As with the continuum from autocratic to democratic on p 12 in Chapter 1, it is possible to erect a similar structure when examining groups and teams taking decisions. This will involve examining some distinct yet interrelated decision-making methods, the majority of which rely for their success on positive relationships among colleagues.

Decisions taken by a single authority

Here the leader simply decides what to do, does it and passes on the results to his or her colleagues. If you think about this method carefully, it is obvious that it is linked to the autocratic end of the autocratic/collegial continuum. There are few advantages to using this method if the relationships involved in working together and teachers being involved in decisions are things that you value. It should be used, however, for legally binding decisions or for directives such as health and safety, fire precautions and medical directives.

Decisions taken by experts

Here, someone with expertise related to the problem has total responsibility for a particular decision. This can be a useful approach if there has been a discussion involving colleagues and a final decision has to be taken. For example, if there have been meetings to look at the progression of skills in art, it will be appropriate for an art 'expert' to make a final decision as to what those skills might be.

Decisions taken by taking everyone's opinion into account

This is certainly a cumbersome process. It means that the leader listens to everyone's opinions and arguments but in the end makes up his or her own mind. If you are one of the people whose views are not taken into account in the final decision it can be off-putting. In decision making, however, there has to be a leader who is able to take the final responsibility. The positive side to this method is that everyone is consulted in some way and at the very least everyone's opinion is heard.

Decisions taken by the minority

When a large team is working to solve a problem or to make changes, there are often sub-groups who have some delegated responsibilities. A good example is the governing body, where there might be a finance committee, a premises committee and a personnel committee, among other sub-groups, who will have some responsibility for taking decisions. This method will only work if the whole larger group accepts that it is a process that they agree with and that the decisions taken will be binding. Its main disadvantage is that the decisions taken may not reflect the views of the majority.

Decisions taken by the majority

This is not as usual as it might appear. It will depend on some kind of ballot or vote, or other method of finding out what the majority decision is. The problem is that there may not be a majority viewpoint. If this is the case, some other method will have to be used. If it does work, it will allow everyone to be involved and can lead to lasting change.

Decisions taken by consensus

This is probably the best way to take decisions but it is also the most time consuming and the most difficult, and that is why it is used less often than it probably should be. It involves agreement through long discussion and negotiation, with a real sharing of ideas and opinions. It is very effective if difficult decisions have to be taken that involve all the staff. It is also true to say that while consensus is an ideal, consent to accept an idea and go along with it will still work well and lead to effective decisions being taken.

Summary of decision making

Teams are built and relationships formed so that colleagues can work together, solve problems and take decisions. Doing this effectively will make the school run smoothly and allow changes to be made successfully and with the least disruption. A decision by a single authority figure will support and be supported by an autocratic management structure, but, as has been suggested before, will also be necessary in the case of decisions about health and safety in a collegial and more democratic management structure.

Consensus and majority decisions are effective when it is important to get as much approval as possible by colleagues. Many issues, such as teaching styles, curriculum planning and classroom management, would benefit from the kind of decision-making process where whole groups, whole departments or, in small schools, whole staffs are involved. However, unlike authority decisions, which do have their place in a collegial structure, majority decisions and consensus seem to have little place in the structures created within an autocratic regime.

HOW GROUPS AND TEAMS ARE SUCCESSFUL

The effective school will be able to respond to criticism and resolve conflict successfully and quickly. This will lead to more honest relationships and the ability to discuss issues openly, without the fear of opening up some area of dispute that will fester for a long period and not only undermine the relationships between colleagues but make it more difficult for teachers to work together to raise standards.

We must face up to the fact that within every school there will be conflict of some kind. There are bound to be different points of view, different ways of working, different personalities and differences in terms of status and power. But, as Everard and Morris in *Effective School Management* suggest, 'conflict in the sense of an honest difference of opinion resulting from the availability of two or more alternative courses of action is not only unavoidable but also a valuable part of life. It helps to ensure that different possibilities are properly considered' (1985: 80). If these differences are managed well, the relationships between colleagues can change and grow. If, however, there is no conflict and no differences of opinion and everything remains the same, there will be stagnation and the danger that there may be an abdication of responsibility, a lack of interest and perhaps lazy thinking. While recognising that conflict may lead to positive and useful problem solving and change, it can also destroy relationships within a school if left unchecked. We all need to know what the best styles of conflict resolution are and how best we can understand the impact that differences of opinion have on how groups of people work productively together. A cooperative and collaborative working atmosphere will enable all teachers

48

to cope more readily with the stresses of working in schools. Everard and Morris continue the idea of collaboration and collegiality as ways to promote positive relationships in school when they suggest that avoiding conflict can be achieved if all teachers have a 'collective responsibility for the interests of the school' and if 'participative decision taking in which the views of interested parties are sought out before coming to a decision' is the norm (1985: 88)

RESOLVING CONFLICT

It has to be repeated again and again that no matter how mature, friendly, professional and sophisticated the relationships are in any school, there will always be conflict. The usual ways of dealing with it are:

❏ ignoring it;
❏ imposing a solution;
❏ facilitating a process where all those involved work out a solution either within their group, team, department or Key Stage, or with the help of an external facilitator.

Of course, ignoring conflict won't work and if it is suppressed it will appear elsewhere in a different and probably more destructive form. If a solution is imposed in an authoritarian way without caring much about the participants' views or feelings, the conflict will remain simmering, ready to break out again. The best solution is to facilitate a solution, but like many of the issues in this chapter, this is not only the best way but also the most difficult and most time consuming, because it involves discussion, compromise, consensus and the ability of colleagues to listen to each other.

Some people are better at conflict resolution than others. Table 2.7 is a long activity which is designed to help you find out your preferred style of handling conflict. It will also suggest how good you are at maintaining relationships within your school. It is adapted from Smith (1996a: 11). It is easy to complete and can be used with all the teaching staff of any school.

It involves choosing, from 30 pairs of statements, the one in each case which best fits your preferred style of handling differences between you and colleagues. It relies on similar statements being paired in different ways, and any repetition is deliberate.

As soon as (a) or (b) has been ringed for each of the statements 1–30, the score grid needs to be completed. For each of the numbers 1–30 circle the same letter you put a ring round on your questionnaire. When this is

Table 2.7 *Styles of conflict resolution*

Read each pair and put a ring round either (a) or (b) in each case.
1. (a) I feel that most things are not worth arguing about, so I don't bother and stick to my own views
   (b) I always try to meet the other person halfway
2. (a) I usually try to find some compromise solution
   (b) I usually pursue my goals firmly without much deviation
3. (a) I like to meet other people halfway
   (b) I like to try to cooperate with other people and follow their ideas
4. (a) If I adopt my own position, I will defend it strongly
   (b) I like to try to cooperate with other people and follow their ideas
5. (a) I usually pursue my goals firmly without much deviation
   (b) I attempt to get all concerns and issues out into the open, especially my own
6. (a) I like to accept the views of other people rather than cause problems
   (b) I avoid colleagues with strong views
7. (a) I usually try to find a compromise solution
   (b) I often sacrifice my own wishes for the wishes of other people
8. (a) I like to get all concerns and issues out into the open
   (b) I usually feel that differences of opinion are not worth worrying about.
9. (a) I prefer to avoid arguments and look for the best solutions
   (b) I always like to meet the other person halfway
10. (a) I like to get all concerns and issues out into the open
    (b) I usually try to find a compromise solution
11. (a) I always like to meet the other person halfway
    (b) If I adopt my own position I will defend it strongly
12. (a) I always like to cooperate with other people and try to follow their ideas
    (b) I feel that most things are not worth arguing about so I don't bother and stick to my own views
13. (a) I am always open and frank and invite other people to behave in the same way
    (b) When there are conflicts I make every effort to win my case
14. (a) I like to accept the views of other people rather than cause problems
    (b) If conflict is causing problems, I often support the middle ground
15. (a) I think cooperation is an excellent idea and I follow other people's ideas
    (b) I prefer to avoid arguments and try to find the best possible solutions

---

16. (a) I prefer to avoid problems and find the best possible solutions
     (b) I think that most things are not worth arguing about so I don't bother and stick to my own views
17. (a) When there are conflicts, I make every effort to win my case
     (b) I avoid colleagues with strong views
18. (a) I usually pursue my goals firmly without much deviation
     (b) I often sacrifice my own wishes for the wishes of other people
19. (a) When there are conflicts I make every effort to win my case
     (b) If a conflict is causing a problem I often support the middle ground
20. (a) If I adopt my own position I will defend it strongly
     (b) I prefer to avoid arguments and try and find the best possible solution
21. (a) I like to accept the views of other people rather than cause problems
     (b) When there are conflicts I make every effort to win my case
22. (a) I often sacrifice my own wishes for the wishes of other people
     (b) I usually feel that differences of opinion are not always worth worrying about
23. (a) I am always open and frank and invite other people to behave in the same way
     (b) I like to accept the views of other people rather than behave in the same way
24. (a) If a conflict is causing problems I like to support the middle ground
     (b) I avoid colleagues with strong views
25. (a) I think that most things are not worth arguing about so I don't bother and stick to my own views
     (b) If I adopt my own position, I will defend it strongly
26. (a) I usually feel that differences of opinion are not always worth worrying about
     (b) I usually pursue my goals firmly without much deviation
27. (a) I avoid colleagues with strong views
     (b) I am always open and frank and invite other people to behave in the same way
28. (a) I usually feel that differences of opinion are not always worth worrying about
     (b) I usually try to find a compromise solution
29. (a) I am always open and frank and invite other people to behave in the same way
     (b) If conflict is causing problems, I often support the middle ground
30. (a) I often sacrifice my own wishes for the wishes of other people
     (b) I like to get all concerns and issues out into the open

Score grid

	A	B	C	D	E
1	a		b		
2			a	b	
3		b	a		
4		b		a	
5				a	b
6	b	a			
7		b	a		
8	b				a
9			b		a
10			b		a
11			a	b	
12	b	a			
13				b	a
14		a	b		
15		a			b
16	b				a
17	b			a	
18		b		a	
19			b	a	
20				a	b
21		a		b	
22	b	a			
23		b			a
24	b		a		
25	a			b	
26	a			b	
27	a				b
28	a		b		
29		b			a
30		a			b
Total number of circled items					

completed, you then need to add the number of circles in each of the columns A–E and write the total in the TOTAL box for each column. The column with the highest number will suggest your dominant style for handling conflict. If you have close scores in two columns, it may mean that you use both styles. Read the description of your dominant style carefully. It is also useful to read all the styles.

There are other interesting questionnaires in: Pedlar *et al* (1986) and Rowland and Birkett (1992).

Now read your favoured style for conflict resolution. Don't forget to read all the other styles as well.

A. Non-assertive style   This means that you prefer not to tackle the conflict and your behaviour is both unassertive and usually uncooperative. At worst, this style means that you will withdraw from any potentially threatening situations but it is possible for you sometimes to wait for a better time and more appropriate opportunity to discuss the issue. If and when conflict does arise, some of your responses might include: 'I'd prefer not to discuss that now. Can't we talk about it later?' 'That is really nothing to do with me.'

B. Agreeing style   This is usually unassertive but usually reasonably cooperative. You will put down and ignore your own needs and concerns to satisfy and meet the needs of your colleagues. You will probably spend a lot of time agreeing when you don't really want to, as well as giving in to your colleagues' points of view and demands. Some of your responses in a conflict situation might include: 'Yes, I totally agree with you.' 'Yes, you've got a good point there and I agree with it.' 'Yes, you have certainly convinced me.'

C. Compromising style   This lies somewhere between being unassertive and being cooperative. You will work hard at finding ways to satisfy all parties who are in conflict with each other. It will possibly mean making concessions and meeting people halfway rather than insisting on all your own way. Some of your likely responses will include: 'I could agree with you there if you would accept that . . . .' 'Let's see if we can agree on some things.' 'If we can agree on this, we will be able to find a quick solution.'

D. Competitive style   This mans that you will behave in an assertive, rather uncooperative way. You will use your own power and expertise to pursue your own concerns in any conflict situation. This will usually mean that you will either attempt to win, defend your own particular position or stand up for your own rights. Your responses could include: 'Let me make my position quite clear.' 'Look, I know my way is the right way.' 'If you don't agree with this I will have to . . .'

E. Problem-solving style   This is where you are both assertive and cooperative. You will aim to resolve a conflict by reaching a solution that satisfies
both persons. To adopt this style, you will need considerable interpersonal
skills, honesty and a willingness to listen to different points of view.
Responses might include: 'Look, it will be better if we all work together on
this.' 'I feel this way about the problem . . . how do you feel?' 'Let's work
out how we can solve this.'

Obviously, it is possible to operate within all the styles suggested, although
successful staff relationships and better conflict resolution and problem
solving will occur with some styles more than others. The *problem-solving
style* will be the most effective and it is one that we should all be able to
use. Conflict and any subsequent breakdown in relationships will make
the school less effective. Solving a problem often involves finding a new
way of sorting out differences between colleagues without putting anyone
in a win–lose situation. This will involve negotiation, discussion and mutual
respect in a way that keeps the issue and the individuals separate. All those
who are involved have to be willing to be assertive but at the same time
feel able to listen to each other, want to find a solution and be prepared to
look at a variety of alternatives.

ASSERTIVENESS

Rowland and Birkett (1992) see assertiveness as the key to managing schools
more effectively and as an important way for teachers to take control of
their own behaviour and how they relate to colleagues in a successful and
professional way:

> Being assertive means . . . having respect for ourselves and others, and
> being honest. It allows us to say what we want and feel but not at
> other people's expense. It means understanding the point of view of
> other people, and being self confident and positive. It is not about
> winning come what may or getting your own way all the time.
> Assertiveness is about handling conflict and coming to an acceptable
> compromise.
>
> (1992: 6)

The rights of assertiveness

In effective schools, everyone recognises that all colleagues have the right
to:

❑ have and express feelings and opinions;
❑ be listened to and taken seriously;
❑ set priorities;
❑ say 'no' without being made to feel guilty;
❑ ask for what they want;
❑ ask for and get information from each other;
❑ sometimes make mistakes.

These 'rights' will help colleagues to feel confident and to feel more in control of decisions and actions. Assertiveness is an important right but it does not come easily to many people and yet it can, at a simple level that needs expanding, be learnt.

A practical guide to assertion

There are times when everyone needs to be assertive. In school, this can be when someone wants you to do something that you are either not happy with, have no time to complete properly, or feel that what you are being asked to do is at the expense of other things that are more important and will lead to higher standards. The kind of responses you make and the action you take are important. They must not be aggressive and must invite a professional, adult response which does not raise anyone's hackles. The responses used in Table 2.8 are based on the following scenario. You receive a memo (this can be a face-to-face request if you like) from the headteacher telling you that he or she is unable to attend a particular meeting and that you will have to go instead because the school needs representing. However, because of the short notice and prior commitments you also cannot go.

It is possible to 'learn' how to respond in an assertive way by using the six stages. This will mean that you are less likely to be taken unawares by requests that you cannot possibly respond to effectively.

THE POSITIVE COLLEAGUE

It is important that colleagues view themselves and each other positively. The positive colleague and especially the positive manager will behave in the following ways. They will:

❑ act rather than remain passive;
❑ accept responsibility;

Table 2.8 *Step-by-step guide to assertion*

Step 1: *Summarise* the problem carefully, factually, unemotionally and straightforwardly; eg 'What you have asked about the meeting tomorrow has caused me considerable problems . . .'

Step 2: *State* exactly how you feel . . . not how anyone else must feel; eg 'I feel very concerned that although it is an important meeting, I will not be able to go.'

Step 3: *Describe* clearly and simply why you feel that way and why you are unable to respond in the way that is wanted; eg 'First of all, I have already arranged a meeting with (colleague X) after school tomorrow and then I am expected home because we have tickets for the theatre.'

Step 4: *Sympathise or empathise* with the other person's point of view or position; eg 'I can understand that it is important for someone to go to the meeting but I am committed to doing other things on that evening.'

Step 5: *Specify* exactly what you would like to happen. It is important to try to find a solution or compromise in the situation; eg 'If it is impossible for either of us to be there, why not telephone a colleague at another school and ask them to collect any information they can. We will be able to collect it at the end of the week.'

Step 6: *Decide* what your final response will be. It is important that this is not threatening; eg 'I think that this solution will work reasonably well. I am sorry that I cannot go but I have already made other arrangements.'

- ❑ be objective;
- ❑ listen and respond;
- ❑ suggest solutions to problems;
- ❑ delegate if it is within their capacity;
- ❑ see opportunities for improvement;
- ❑ have a breadth of vision that will lead to more effective practice;
- ❑ face up to problems;
- ❑ continue to learn;
- ❑ have foresight.

Table 2.9 *Positive or negative colleagues*

1. 'I'm OK, you're OK': This means everyone gets along together and should mean that the relationships within the school are such that change, decision making and collegiality are relatively easy to do well.
2. 'I'm OK, you're not OK': This is how you get rid of people and in many ways it is the selfish colleague getting his or her own way. There will be little working together and decisions taken in this way, where the majority are unlikely to agree, will be resented. On the level of individual relationships, it means that one colleague wins at the expense of another.
3. 'I'm not OK, you're OK': This is where you can feel isolated because everyone else seems to be achieving what they want and need and yet you are not achieving anything or getting anything out of the situation.
4. 'I'm not OK, you're not OK': This is where the relationships are such that no one is getting anywhere and no one is relating to anyone else. This is obviously an intolerable position where nothing will happen and where decisions will never be taken.

Positive relationships

How colleagues relate to each other is extremely important because the success of working together depends on the effectiveness of the whole group. Everyone knows that some people are easier to work with than others.

The positive and the negative colleague

The positive colleague will be easy to work with and generally cooperative and responsive. The negative colleague, however, will be relatively difficult to work with and is more likely to be a poor team member, indifferent and wanting his or her own way. Table 2.9 suggests a useful summary of attitudes and relationships from Montgomery (1989). She suggests that there are four positions that describe whether behaviour is positive or negative.

In Table 2.9, it should be apparent that holding a position such as that in number 1 will suggest sharing, good communications and a general feeling of professional respect and equality. Others such as number 2 are less effective positions to hold and, in fact, numbers 3 and 4 will be disruptive and largely ineffective. To be 'OK' and for your colleagues to be 'OK' and to work in a school with positive relationships takes time and effort. It is not an automatic situation, even though it is the only one that will raise standards and make the school successful.

Criteria for effective professional relationships

The following criteria have to exist in order for 'effectiveness' and 'success' to be the norm. If they don't exist in your school, it is important to ask yourself what needs to happen to make them exist. Colleagues need to behave in the following ways:

- ❑ Keep the discussions going if there is a tendency not to discuss teaching and learning.
- ❑ Support other people's points of view by saying the right things and behaving appropriately.
- ❑ Invite all colleagues to contribute to discussions and working groups.
- ❑ Ask questions that take colleagues forward.
- ❑ Offer advice about where to look for further information and ideas.

Negative teacher behaviour

Within any school, and this has been stressed earlier in the chapter, there are bound to be teachers who are negative, who have problems sustaining the effort of discussing important issues and who find the whole business of moving forward and raising standards difficult and threatening. One person's negative reactions can have quite a devastating effect on decisions, forward planning and change. It is difficult to suggest how you can change colleagues who behave in this way. One step, however, is by beginning to recognise what they actually do.

Blocking tactics

Many colleagues who are nervous of change or who feel threatened by the intellectual nature of how schools can be made to be more effective often create a kind of internal block and shut out their awareness of any problems. In trying to avoid the important issue they may well build up distracting points that are relatively meaningless to the task in hand. What they all

Table 2.10 *Blocking tactics*

❏ We shouldn't spend too much time working together when we all have our own responsibilities.
❏ We tried that before and it didn't work then, so why should it work now?
❏ We don't need to talk about the jobs we do all the time. We should just do them without having to think about them.
❏ I don't need to listen to anyone else's ideas as I know mine are good ones.
❏ It may have worked somewhere else but it won't work here.
❏ Aren't we all too busy to take on any new ideas at the moment?
❏ We won't receive enough help for us to change to that way of working
❏ What a strange idea! Don't you think that it is too far divorced from reality?
❏ Why do we need to change when everything seems to be working· fine?
❏ I've been teaching for 20 years and you can't teach an old dog new tricks.
❏ I am sure that some of us might think that is a good idea, but isn't it a bit impractical?
❏ Well I suppose s/he means well but . . . .
❏ Don't you think that this will have an adverse effect on the children? Are we really thinking of them?
❏ I remember reading something about this and I thought it was ridiculous then.
❏ That's fine, but can we give it some more thought?
❏ We'd be a laughing stock if we did this
❏ Oh, not that old idea again!
❏ Are we sure that this idea will work? Has it been tried anywhere else?
❏ I'm sure the parents and governors won't like it.

have in common, however, is a list of 'blocking' phrases that will take all the powers of assertion, leadership and team building to neutralise. Table 2.10 illustrates a sample of such phrases, which are usually made when individuals are working together in groups or teams. It is useful to try to suggest how you would counteract some or all of the tactics.

In an effective school, individual colleagues should have a positive effect on each other. It is true that in some instances some of the statements in Table 2.10 are quite reasonable. If a positive colleague, for example, suggests 'That's fine, but can we give it some thought?', it may lead to further discussion. On the other hand, the same statement coming from a colleague with a reputation for negative behaviour would be seen as suggesting that the idea under discussion hadn't really been thought through. You have to be able to listen and move through such irrelevancies and unhelpful points towards a successful end product. Tasks have to be completed, standards have to be raised and everyone has to participate in some area of the school, and it is important that relationships between colleagues are taken into account. Everyone working in a school has to make sure that they influence others positively by assertive persuasion, participation, trust and a common vision rather than by their own dictatorial aggression.

IMPORTANT POINTS

❑ Positive relationships with colleagues are obviously important and will influence the smooth running of the school and the success of any changes that have to be managed. If we all look at how we relate to what we are expected to do and our relationships with each other, we will recognise strengths and be able to face up to problems and weaknesses.

❑ This chapter has explored the characteristics of positive and 'good' working relationships. It has given examples of the importance of teams working together to solve problems and initiate change without losing sight of the difficulties that groups and teams have when they work together to improve or change what already exists.

❑ Colleagues in school have many foibles and consist of individuals with many different attitudes and personalities. Leading teams is difficult, and how decisions are managed in these circumstances can be complicated and depend to a large extent on the level of maturity of the relationships between colleagues. This level of maturity is reflected in how conflict is managed successfully and how assertive behaviour is an important way that an individual can work within a team and, at the same time, maintain their individuality at a level that will benefit themselves and the whole team.

❑ There are various lists of attributes and working behaviours in this chapter. At the risk of repeating some of them, here is a final list of examples of good practice. If your school is to be effective and if the

relationships between colleagues are to continue to be positive, every-one will:
- spend time planning and reflecting;
- discuss what is happening in the school;
- recognise new ideas to which the school should be receptive;
- be aware of what is happening in education both locally and nationally;
- have faith in colleagues' abilities;
- be optimistic and positive;
- be imaginative;
- refuse to be complacent;
- be good at listening;
- surround themselves with effective colleagues;
- enjoy other people's accomplishments;
- be a good communicator;
- be open minded and supportive.

3

THE CURRICULUM AND RAISING PUPIL ACHIEVEMENT

This chapter looks at:

❏ identifying the curriculum;
❏ the curriculum: content and process;
❏ whole school curriculum policy;
❏ key whole school curriculum principles;
❏ curriculum planning;
❏ levels of planning;
❏ levels of curriculum planning.

It considers the importance of the curriculum and the ways in which school leaders can plan it effectively.

IDENTIFYING THE CURRICULUM

Effective schools will have a shared curriculum vision that all teachers understand and work with, but before we develop a more sophisticated identification of what the curriculum actually is, let's create a basic definition of what is quite a difficult concept. *A Curriculum for All* (NCA, 1989) opens with the sentence: 'All pupils share the right to a broad and balanced curriculum' (1989: 1). Elton (DES, 1989) states: 'On the curriculum there are issues at three levels. First the National Curriculum, second the curricula offered by individual schools and thirdly the curricula offered by individual pupils.' (1989: 103) It is surprising that Elton, despite the dominance of the National Curriculum, manages to include the rights of both schools and individual pupils to have some say in what is to be taught and learnt. In the days preceding the National Curriculum, the *Curriculum from 5–16* (HMI, 1985) suggests that: 'All pupils should have access to a curriculum of similar breadth and balance irrespective of their level of ability' (1985: 24). Finally, one of the statements in the *Handbook for Inspecting Primary and Nursery Schools* (OFSTED, 2000) which they say applies to a very good to excellent school is: 'The curriculum interprets statutory requirements in stimulating as well as structured ways, providing for high achievement, particularly in core subjects, and offering pupils a wealth of additional opportunities' (2000: 66)

All these definitions stress a broad and balanced core of knowledge and stress that the curriculum that is taught belongs to the state, the school and the child. Whatever we say about the curriculum, we have to be able to share our vision with all our colleagues. This culture of sharing relates back to Chapters 1 and 2, because it will vary from school to school. At one extreme might be the school with headteacher-driven initiatives and at the other, the inclusive collegiate approach. In order to deliver an effective curriculum, information needs to be shared and there needs to be the kind of leadership that encourages a shared understanding of, and an active participation in, the creation of the curriculum aims of the school.

THE CURRICULUM: CONTENT AND PROCESS

The broad definitions used so far have been mainly to do with the content, and such terms as breadth, balance, core subjects, etc, have been used. Of equal importance, however, are the processes that help pupils learn. They will include:

❏   how the curriculum is taught;
❏   what teaching styles are used;
❏   how the classroom is managed.

(All three areas are discussed in detail in Chapter 5.)

A successful school will focus on the curriculum as the 'public face of the school'. This will include its subjects, its classroom teaching styles and its treatment of the content of the curriculum, bearing in mind that a large part of this will be the National Curriculum. At the same time, it is also important to bear in mind that there is this hidden and more private curriculum of processes, of how children are treated and the importance of teachers as models for the values they wish to communicate to their pupils.

Table 3.1 identifies five curriculum areas which represent five common characteristics of an effective curriculum in terms of both content and process.

Table 3.1 *Curriculum characteristics*

---

1. Breadth

The Education Reform Act (1998), which introduced the National Curriculum, suggested that it should be broad and balanced. In schools where the curriculum does have breadth and a wide range of subjects and extra-curricular activities, there seems to be higher achievement in basic skills.

2. Balance

Different aspects of the curriculum need to be given an appropriate weight of time. What was recognised in *Curriculum Organisation and Classroom Practice in primary Schools: A Follow up Report* (DfEE, 1993) was that: 'if schools were over stretched to provide the National Curriculum, depth was likely to be sacrificed in pursuit of breadth. The aim should be to strike a better balance than currently existed which meant attempting less but doing it more thoroughly' (1993: 15—16)

3. Relevance

What is learnt in school needs to be recognised by pupils as having some relevance. All pupils need to be told why they are learning things, and it is important that they understand the objectives behind lessons.

4. Differentiation

The curriculum has to be matched to the needs of each class, cohort or year of pupils as well as to the individual child. Teachers who are aware of the need to differentiate are also aware that pupils need to be challenged at the most suitable level. This match of task to ability means that pupils learn effectively.

5. Progression and continuity

The curriculum needs to be seen as a whole, and teachers should have an idea of what happens at all stages in their own school.

It should be possible to see the links between a broad curriculum and the school aims statement (see Chapter 1, p 6). They should join together to form an umbrella under which the school operates. The success of whatever curriculum is planned, however, will depend on teachers adopting a style of classroom management that is able to cope with a variety of learning styles as well as the range of pupils' strengths and weaknesses.

Management issues affecting the curriculum

When identifying the curriculum, there are several key management issues that will affect what is taught. They will include:

❏ **Entitlement** – There needs to be an assumption that pupils are entitled to certain things, such as a broad and balanced curriculum which will draw on their individual talents. A major management concern might be that the National Curriculum plus the concentration on literacy and numeracy force schools to push breadth and balance to the side and concentrate solely on the core subjects, with little time left for the foundation subjects.

❏ **Consensus** – There has to be consensus that the curriculum, in terms of what is taught, can be resourced in terms of teacher time, training and the necessary hardware such as books, computers, etc.

❏ **Professionalism** – Professional control over the content of the curriculum has largely been taken away from teachers and they have been left with interpreting a nationally laid down curriculum framework. Motivating staff to identify what their children need and what they need to be taught has to be central to any debate and any decisions that are taken about what the curriculum actually is.

❏ **Responsiveness** – Success in teaching is partly dependent on recognising that the curriculum needs to start from the child's own knowledge, that is, where a child is on the curriculum ladder at a particular time and place. Teachers need to be able to respond to the needs of the children they teach within the breadth and balance of their curriculum, rather than within the narrow constraints of an imposed curriculum.

WHOLE SCHOOL CURRICULUM POLICY

It has been an assumption from the start of this chapter that the curriculum aims of your school are accepted and understood by all teachers and, hopefully, teaching assistants. There are two basic aims to the curriculum that can act as a starting point: 1) it should aim to provide opportunities for all pupils to learn and achieve; 2) it should aim to promote pupils' spiritual, moral and cultural development and prepare all pupils for the opportunities, responsibilities and experiences of life.

Table 3.2 *Questions about curricular provision*

---

1. Does the school have a current and up-to-date curriculum statement which everyone, including governors, understands and approves?
2. What kind of statement of the time needed for each subject over a period of a week and a year do you have?
3. What provision is there for 'peripheral' subjects such as PSHE, Religious Education and Modern Languages?
4. What provision is there for making sure that children with SEN are catered for?
5. What part does the curriculum play in ensuring that respect, tolerance and good behaviour are part of the school's culture?

Table 3.2 suggests some of the questions that each school needs to ask as they begin to prepare their whole school policy or as they are reviewing their existing policy statements.

KEY WHOLE SCHOOL CURRICULUM PRINCIPLES

In primary education, there need to be key principles which apply to all pupils and to the whole curriculum. These need to be considered and should form the background to any statements about the curriculum in the school's curriculum policy.

These key principles will be that schools and all who work in them should always aim to:

❑ know what their basic and unchanging values are;
❑ have, as an umbrella, equality of opportunity, entitlement and access to the whole curriculum;
❑ build relationships in the school;
❑ create an ethos of maintaining and improving self-esteem;
❑ make sure that there is always a framework of mutual respect;
❑ create and implement a culture of achievement, success and high expectations;
❑ offer a broad and balanced curriculum that prepares pupils for their next stage of education;
❑ encourage independent learning;

❑ build on pupils' natural curiosity and their thirst for learning;
❑ celebrate achievements;
❑ raise standards;
❑ allow time for high quality in-depth work;
❑ allow time for periods of reflection.

The curriculum statement

Chapter 6 begins with several important statements by OFSTED about the curriculum. In developing a general curriculum statement that is as relevant for an OFSTED inspection as it is for teachers and parents, it is important to bear these statements in mind. In your school's curriculum statement, however, there is no need to go into great detail about OFSTED's expectations, nor is it necessary to make elaborate comments about each subject that is taught. This is the job of individual coordinators who will produce a subject policy statement which is relevant to both teachers and inspectors. However, it would be a foolish school whose general curriculum policy statement did not take into account much of what OFSTED see as the provision necessary for a successful, good and/or very good school (see Chapter 6, p 149)

Table 3.3 is the start of a brief summary of a school curriculum statement. There will be more added to it later in the chapter. It is not a definitive statement and it can be used as a starting point for a new statement or the review of an existing one.

A positive curriculum for all children and for the whole school

A positive curriculum will contain many, if not all of the attributes that have been discussed so far in this chapter, but it will also allow children to:

❑ integrate prior and new knowledge;
❑ acquire and use a wide range of thinking and learning skills;
❑ solve problems individually and in groups;
❑ reflect on their experiences in order to make sense of what they have learnt and consider how it fits into their lives now and in the future;
❑ respond to new opportunities and challenges.

In providing a relevant and stimulating curriculum which has a positive effect on standards and learning, we shouldn't overlook the fact that it needs

Table 3.3 *An example of a curriculum statement*

We aim to deliver a high quality education to all children.
We will do this by providing a well-balanced curriculum, which will be:

❏ broad and balanced, based on the requirements of the National Curriculum;
❏ stimulating and challenging in a way that will extend children's knowledge, skills and creativity in order to develop enquiring minds;
❏ committed to the principle of equality for all children;
❏ relevant to the needs and interests of all children;
❏ able to provide all children with the skills to develop their potential intellectually, physically and emotionally;
❏ able to allow each child to question, acquire self-knowledge and develop independence;
❏ able to provide children with the opportunity to develop their own self-esteem.

The curriculum will be taught using a variety of teaching styles and groupings, as appropriate to the intellectual and emotional development of the needs of the children.
All children will be provided with opportunities to learn from a wide range of experiences.
All teaching will be planned to develop individuals' potential and will take account of both previous and future learning needs.
Children will have regular and constructive feedback about their work.
All children will, commensurate with their ability and maturity, be expected to evaluate their work and social relationships in order to improve personal standards and enhance relationships.

to be holistic, in the sense that pupils are expected to have fun by progressing through a range of learning experiences and skill development, including extra-curricular activities and those that are able to be linked to the wider community. Achieving these kinds of high expectations will depend on effective curriculum planning based on high expectations, setting appropriate targets and assessing that the targets have been met.

CURRICULUM PLANNING

A good curriculum is one that is organised and planned appropriately and effectively in terms of time allocation to subjects. It will include grouping arrangements which enable all pupils to achieve their full potential across the range of National Curriculum subjects, RE and PSHE together with a modern foreign language.

A less effective or even 'bad' curriculum will lack one or more important features, such as breadth, balance, differentiation or relevance for some of the pupils. It will not have been planned as a whole, with any provision for continuity and achievement. Opportunities for promoting essential knowledge, skills and understanding may have been neglected, and the time allocations for some subjects will be inadequate for the work that has to be covered.

It is important to make sure that all subjects are present within the curriculum plan and that they are available for all pupils. The distribution of time between subjects will be a factor in judging the effectiveness of the school's curricular planning. It is also very important that what the school says in its documentation, eg the curriculum statement, and what actually happens in practice in long-, medium- and short-term planning, can be seen to be the same thing.

LEVELS OF PLANNING

The three levels of curriculum planning that are important are:

❑ long term, ie a whole Key Stage;
❑ medium term, which is usually a term or half-term;
❑ short term, which will be a week or, in extreme cases, a day.

Curriculum expectations in the planning process

When considering the broad curricular aims of your school, it is essential that account is taken of both what you want to teach and what you want the children to achieve. One way of doing this, before any planning takes place, is to say: as a school, we expect all pupils to experience achievement and to reach potential in the following areas:

1. **Academic achievement** – Pupils must be able to write, respond appropriately, remember without having to look everything up and able to organise the material that they are using.
2. **Applying knowledge** – They must be able to deal with practical as well as theoretical knowledge and the spoken as well as the written word. Problem solving and the skills of investigation are important when applying knowledge.
3. **Social and interpersonal skills** – This is the capacity to communicate with others face to face and the ability to cooperate with them. It is about initiative, self-reliance and the ability to work alone without being closely supervised.
4. **Motivation and commitment** – This is about being able to persevere, learning in spite of difficulties and being willing to try new things.
5. **Decision making and independent learning** – Individuals need to be able to exercise choice, take decisions and express their own points of view.
6. **Equal opportunities** – The curriculum will expect all children to adopt a positive attitude towards a multiracial society as well as learning to appreciate other people's right to be different.

In many ways these are learning processes rather than the content of what has to be learnt. Such processes will not only be defined by the school's ethos and attitudes but also help determine what these will be.

The effect on curriculum planning of what pupils know

It is difficult to be totally effective in ensuring pace, rigour and challenge for able pupils and at the same time make sure that low achievers complete work with understanding and enjoyment. This is true of all tiers of planning, but becomes more important the closer you are to what children actually do in the classroom, which is the key to curriculum planning. The observation and recording of what children are actually doing lies at the heart of planning a successful curriculum at the level of what is to be taught and what is expected to be learnt. This is the fundamental starting point, and schools must plan in a way that recognises what their pupils can already do and where they need to go next. In fact this needs to dominate long-, medium- and short-term planning.

In trying to decide what issues are important, it is worth considering the following:

❏　What stages do we think our pupils pass through in their development?
❏　There needs to be methods to find what pupils know at one stage before they are passed on to the next.
❏　We need to know about the kinds of activities and approaches that are likely to help pupils take the next step and make progress.
❏　We need to make sure that when children move through the curriculum, we have planned for continuity and progression in the medium and short term.

LEVELS OF CURRICULUM PLANNING

Table 3.4 identifies the planning stage or level together with its purposes and suggested outcomes.

Long-term planning

There have been several key dates when most schools will have reviewed their long-term curriculum map. The first was in 1988–9 when the National Curriculum was first introduced, the second was after the Dearing review in 1995, and the latest was the revised curriculum 2000 which was implemented in September 2000. There are many good reasons for monitoring and evaluating long-term planning regularly. Table 3.5 suggests many of the significant changes that will have affected long-term planning and which have been imposed during the last few years.

All the changes in Table 3.5 are important and represent a considerable amount of work for schools in implementing them. Many teachers will argue that they have come too fast and too soon and that there has been little time to manage one initiative successfully before another one has appeared, even though some resources such as non-statutory guidelines for PSHE, all kinds of numeracy and literacy training and other materials, QCA schemes of work, etc, have been made available to schools to help them implement all the imposed initiatives.

Stages in long-term planning

There are five stages in the planning of the curriculum:

Stage 1　Identify what has to be taught and who will teach it. This will be the National Curriculum plus other national initiatives such as

Table 3.4 *Levels of curriculum planning*

PLANNING LEVEL	STAFF MEMBERS	PURPOSES	OUTCOMES
Long term (for the whole Key Stage)	Headteacher and all staff	To ensure: ❏ coverage of the National Curriculum and all other appropriate 'subjects'; ❏ progression in each subject across the whole Key Stage; ❏ balance within and across subjects in each year of the Key Stage; ❏ balance within and across subjects in each year of the Key Stage; ❏ coherence within and between subjects; ❏ appropriate allocations of time; ❏ appropriate links between subjects; ❏ continuity between Key Stages.	A broad framework for each year of the Key Stage which reflects the school's overall curricular aims and objectives and which: ❏ specifies the content to be taught in each subject; ❏ organises the content into manageable and coherent units of work; ❏ allocates time to each unit of work; ❏ sequences work; ❏ identifies links between aspects of different subjects.
Medium term (for a term or half-term)	Class teachers and planning teams supported by curriculum coordinators	To develop the Key Stage plan for a particular year into a	A detailed specification for each unit of work to be taught within

72

			detailed sequence of subject specific and linked units of work.	the term or half-term which sets out: ❑ specific learning objectives; ❑ priorities and depth of treatment; ❑ links and references to other units of work; ❑ the nature of pupil tasks and activities; ❑ suggested teaching strategies and pupil groupings; ❑ strategies for differentiating work; ❑ assessment opportunities.
Short term (each week or day)	Class teachers	To ensure: ❑ a balance of different kinds of activity throughout a week; ❑ differentiation; ❑ appropriate pace; ❑ constructive feedback for pupils; ❑ time for teacher assessment; ❑ monitoring, evaluation and, if required, modifications to the medium-term plan.	Detailed daily or weekly lesson plans and associated records to ensure effective day-to-day teaching and inform curriculum planning.

Table 3.5 *Curriculum innovations*

Literacy hour
Numeracy strategy
Early learning goals and foundation curriculum
Target setting
PSHE and citizenship
Key skills
School self-review suggestions from Ofsted
Performance management and threshold assessment

RE and PSHE and probably a foreign language such as French, together with any additional learning areas that the school agrees to do.

Stage 2 Identify what needs to be added to the existing curriculum. For example, perhaps PSHE needs to be allocated a specific block of time, does 'circle time' need a time slot, etc. There might be aspects of the work you intend to do with the local community or local secondary schools that you want to emphasise, eg arts and technology projects, links between education and industry.

Stage 3 Look back at decisions you have made relating to the curriculum and the quality of teaching and learning. Do any of these decisions affect how your long-term planning works?

Stage 4 Look at the time analysis that you have in place. Does this need changing? Is there a need to change how the week, half-term, year is organised? (Table 3.6 suggests examples of subject time allocation.)

Stage 5 How will you organise the curriculum content? Questions that need to be asked include:

❏ What worked in the past and how was it organised?
❏ What caused problems?
❏ Is there a different method of organising the curriculum for different subjects?
❏ Is it possible to maintain an overall picture of progression in the skills, knowledge and understanding of each subject?

Other long-term planning routes

The five stages in long-term planning, together with Table 3.6, which is in effect the end product of the long-term planning process, are not the only routes towards an effective curriculum. Table 3.7 suggests some alternatives and does so by asking three rather basic questions:

❏ What needs to happen in the development of the most effective curriculum?
❏ Why will this help us develop the curriculum?
❏ What do we need to consider as we are developing it?

Long-term planning within a curriculum policy

In Table 3.3, there are suggestions as to the content of a school curriculum policy. The resulting policy will have to contain relevant information about the school's intentions regarding long-term planning (Table 3.8). It is important to make sure that the expertise of subject coordinators is drawn upon to initiate schemes of work as a result of the planning process and to help promote continuity between subjects, as well as individual subject integrity where it is appropriate.

Medium-term planning

All schools will have medium-term plans in place and should be looking at them closely in case changes are necessary. It is important, when reviewing them, that the strengths of the school and the expertise of all staff, teachers and teaching assistants are taken into account.

Medium-term planning should be consistent with the school's aims statement, teaching and learning policy, schemes of work and long-term planning.

The content of the medium-term planning together with a structured plan of action can be developed using the following stages of development:

Stage 1 Consider the specific learning objectives and their relationship to the development of the pupils' skills. Also take into account any Individual Education Plans (IEPs) and behaviour support plans.

Stage 2 Consider the links between subjects and the necessary time allocation to avoid marginalising some subject areas.

Stage 3 Consider the resources that are needed and the possibility of using the wider community as a resource.

Stage 4 Consider the learning experiences of what you want your pupils to have. These might include:
   ❏ using skills developed in one subject which are practised and assessed in another subject context;

Table 3.6 *Curriculum time allocation*

Infants

Sessions in the school day	8.55 am–12.00 (3 hrs 5 min) 1.00 pm–3.20 pm (2hrs 20 min)
Total time in school	5 hrs 25 min per day 27 hrs 5 min per week
Breaks	2 hrs 30 min per week
Assembly/collective worship	1 hr 15 min per week
Registration	1 hr per week
Time committed to teaching National Curriculum subjects and other curricular provision (total time in week minus time for breaks/registration and assemblies)	**22 hrs 20min per week**
Number of weeks available in school year	38 weeks (+5 training days)
Special curriculum events and activities which require short blocks of time planned within the appropriate term for individual year groups, eg ❏ end of Key Stage tests; ❏ residential visits; ❏ Christmas activities; ❏ rehearsals; ❏ sports days; ❏ links with local community; ❏ Book week	2 weeks
Remaining weeks committed to teaching the school curriculum	**36 weeks**
Total hours (36 × 22 hrs 20 min)	**804 hours**
Statutory curricular provision	KS1 programmes of study for all NC subjects, Religious education/ PSHE, etc.

Estimated annual curriculum time allocation – Infants

Sub	Eng	Ma	Sc	D&T	ICT	Hi	Geo	Art	Mu	PE	MFL	RE	PSHE	Total
% Time Year 1	26	22	8	4.5	6	4.5	4.5	4.5	4.5	9		3.5	3	100
Av. hours Year 1	210	180	63	36	48	36	36	36	36	72		27	24	804
Av. hours per week Year 1	5.8	5	1.75	1	1.3	1	1	1	1	2		0.75	0.6	22 hrs 20 min
% time Year 2	26	22	8	4.5	6	4.5	4.5	4.5	4.5	9		3.5	3	100
Av. hours Year 2	210	180	63	36	48	36	36	36	36	72		27	24	804
Av. hours per week yr.2	5.8	5	1.75	1	1.3	1	1	1	1	2		0.75	0.66	22 hrs 20 mins

Curriculum time allocation
Juniors

Sessions in the school day	8.55 am–12.15 pm (3 hrs 20 min) 1.15 pm–3.20 pm (2 hrs 5 min)
Total time in school	5 hrs 25 min per day 27 hrs 5 min per week
Breaks (max.with only some pm taken)	2 hrs 5 min per week
Assembly/collective worship	1 hr per week
Registration	45 min per week
Time committed to teaching National Curriculum, RE and other curricular provision (total time minus breaks/assembly/registration)	**23 hrs 15 min**
Number of weeks available during the school year	38 weeks + 5 training days
Special curriculum events and activities which require short blocks of time planned within the appropriate term for individual year groups, eg	2 weeks

❏ end of Key Stage tests; ❏ residential visits; ❏ Christmas parties; ❏ rehearsals; ❏ sports days; ❏ links with local community; ❏ Book week	
Remaining weeks committed to teaching the school curriculum	**36 weeks**
Total hours (36 × 23 hrs 15 min)	**837 hrs**
Statutory curriculum provision	KS2 programmes of study for all National Curriculum subjects, RE and PSHE, etc.

Estimated annual curriculum time allocation – Juniors

Sub	Eng	Ma	Sc	D&T	ICT	Hi	Geo	Art	Mus	PE	MFL	RE	PSHE	Total
% Time year 3	29	21.5	7.5	4.3	4.3	4.3	4.3	4.3	4.3	8.6		3.2	4.3	100
Av. hours Year 3	243	180	63	36	36	36	36	36	36	72		27	36	837
Av. hours per week Year 3	6.75	5	1.75	1	1	1	1	1	1	2		0.75	1	23 hrs 15 min
% Time year 4	29	21.3	7.5	4.3	4.3	4.3	4.3	4.3	4.3	8.6		3.2	4.3	100
Av. hours Year 4	243	180	63	36	36	36	36	36	36	72		27	36	837
Av. hours per week Year 4	5.75	5	1.75	1	1	1	1	1	1	2		0.75	1	23 hrs 15 min
% Time year 5	25	21.5	9.5	4.3	4.3	4.3	4.3	4.3	4.3	8.6	3.2	3.2	3.2	100
Av. hours Year 5	208	180	80	36	36	36	36	36	36	72	27	27	27	837
Av. hours per week Year 5	5.75	5	2.25	1	1	1	1	1	1	2	0.75	0.75	0.75	23 hrs 15 min

% Time Year 6	25	21.5	9.5	4.3	4.3	4.3	4.3	4.3	4.3	8.6	3.2	3.2	3.2	100
Av. hours Year 6	208	180	80	36	36	36	36	36	36	72	27	27	27	837
Av. hours per wk Year 6	5.75	5	2.25	1	1	1	1	1	1	2	0.75	0.75	0.75	23 hrs 15 min

Table 3.7 *Alternative curriculum routes*

WHAT NEEDS TO HAPPEN?	WHY WOULD THIS HELP?	WHAT DO WE NEED TO CONSIDER?
1. Design a weekly timetable.	This would balance the time on a weekly basis.	❏ The short time span might create learning experiences that lack depth. ❏ Time may be lost in changing from one lesson to the next. ❏ There is a lot of pressure on short-term planning.
2. Design a fort-nightly timetable.	This would balance the time and allow for slightly more depth than a weekly plan.	Continuity and progression between lessons may be difficult to maintain.
3. Design a series of cross-curricular themes, eg combining history, geography and science.	There are longer blocks of time for in-depth cross-curricular work which will improve curriculum links.	There are difficulties in tracking coverage and progression in each subject.
4. Subject-focused events such as book week, poetry week, technology week, etc, can be arranged.	There are opportunities to work in depth on specific subjects and areas within subjects, eg work with a visiting artist or dance teacher.	There are bound to be long time gaps between similar experiences.

Table 3.8 *Long-term planning in a curriculum statement*

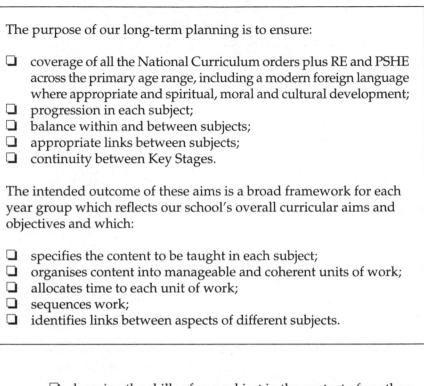

The purpose of our long-term planning is to ensure:

❑ coverage of all the National Curriculum orders plus RE and PSHE across the primary age range, including a modern foreign language where appropriate and spiritual, moral and cultural development;
❑ progression in each subject;
❑ balance within and between subjects;
❑ appropriate links between subjects;
❑ continuity between Key Stages.

The intended outcome of these aims is a broad framework for each year group which reflects our school's overall curricular aims and objectives and which:

❑ specifies the content to be taught in each subject;
❑ organises content into manageable and coherent units of work;
❑ allocates time to each unit of work;
❑ sequences work;
❑ identifies links between aspects of different subjects.

❑ learning the skills of one subject in the context of another;
❑ two or more subjects linked under a theme to enrich another subject area;
❑ linking areas of the curriculum.

Stage 5 Consider which areas of work will be continuous, ie themes and projects involving different subjects and, for example, science or design and technology, which may need a continuous block of several hours as a single subject.

Stage 6 Consider assessment opportunities.

Who needs to know what in medium-term planning

In determining how the medium-term planning should be structured, roles and responsibilities need to be considered. This is because we are beginning to move away from the abstract curriculum map of long-term planning, which is essentially the umbrella under which teaching and learning take place, towards what actually gets taught in classrooms.

Headteachers and senior managers need to know what is happening by:

❑ having an overview across all Key Stages;
❑ monitoring and evaluating samples of work from year groups;
❑ making classroom observations to find out what is actually going on.

Curriculum coordinators need to know about:

❑ standards that are achieved;
❑ continuity and progression;
❑ differentiation;
❑ consistency of 'subject' coverage;
❑ time allocation;
❑ how planning is matched to schemes of work and to the National Curriculum;
❑ the quality of teaching;
❑ the importance of working alongside colleagues;
❑ the kinds of targets that are set by teachers.

Class teachers have the responsibility for translating medium-term planning into weekly and daily plans. In doing this they must take into account such things as IEPs.

Governors have the responsibility for the overall delivery of the curriculum. They must receive information about all kinds of planning issues so that they can fulfil their responsibilities.

Tables 3.3. and 3.8 suggest what should be included in your whole school curriculum policy. Table 3.9 extends this by including examples of what might be added in sections on medium-term planning.

Short-term planning

We have moved from the whole school concept of the long-term curriculum plan, through the year team and groups of teachers working in six-week or whole term blocks of curriculum time to the more personal and individual area of short-term daily and weekly planning. All short-term planning, however, has to have a common structure. It is no good, for example, each teacher creating their own short-term plans without any sense of coherence or common ground. There needs to be a consistent model that everyone follows, and of course it must be based on the content in the medium-term plans.

Table 3.9 *Medium-term planning in the curriculum statement*

Planning
Each year group planning team will develop a detailed plan for a term or half-term. The planning team is led by the year coordinator and should draw upon the expertise of all subject coordinators even if they are not part of a particular team.
    Planning should set out:

❑   learning objectives;
❑   resource requirements, including time;
❑   nature of tasks and activities (learning experiences);
❑   links to other areas of work where appropriate;
❑   suggested teaching strategies and pupil groupings;
❑   assessment opportunities;
❑   strategies for differentiation;
❑   evaluation.

Monitoring
Each year team member will have a copy of the medium-term plan. Two further sets of plans are sent to the headteacher. One set is distributed to relevant subject coordinators, and verbal and written feedback is given to each planning team. Subject coordinators may ask for examples of finished units of work to assist them in their role in monitoring the curriculum. Senior staff trawl curriculum areas on a formal basis once a year and core subject coordinators produce appropriate action plans from the discussion of work.

Evaluation
At the end of each term, each year group will meet to evaluate the success of the term's medium-term planning. At the start of the next term, a written evaluation is handed to the headteacher by the year team.

Involving parents
At the beginning of each block of work, year teams will inform parents by letter of the main focus of the forthcoming work.

If long-term planning is about years (for example, a four-year cycle of work is common in many Junior schools), and medium-term planning is about a term or half-term, then short-term planning is about a day or a week. It is about what I am going to teach today at 9.00 am or on Thursday at 11.00 am.

Some of the features of a short-term plan are as follows:

❑ It is a working document that individual teachers will use.
❑ It is a link between planning and practice.
❑ It should set down aspects of what is to be taught and make the work of teachers and assistants more effective.
❑ The short-term plan should set clear objectives for each lesson.
❑ It should make clear the kinds of skills, knowledge and understanding that are going to be taught.
❑ Assessment that will inform future planning should be built into the short-term plan.
❑ Differentiation should also be built in.

In preparing short-term plans, it should be possible to meet the needs of all pupils as well as the demands set by the curriculum. This does not mean, however, that there needs to be an enormous amount of detail. It should only be necessary to include the following:

❑ clear learning objectives;
❑ teaching and learning experiences;
❑ assessment opportunities;
❑ how differentiation will be organised;
❑ time organisation of the week and/or day;
❑ how the week's work will be reviewed;
❑ the resources that will be used.

Tables 3.3, 3.8 and 3.9 suggest what should be written in your curriculum policy statement. Table 3.10 adds to this by including aspects of short-term planning.

IMPORTANT POINTS

This chapter has identified all the main ingredients that make up the curriculum recipe. It has suggested that the content of what is to be taught and the process, which is how it is taught, are both vital to the success of

Table 3.10 *Short-term planning in the curriculum statement*

Short-term planning translates medium-term planning into lesson plans which are appropriately for a particular class or group.
  The short-term planning will ensure that there is:

❑ a focus on learning objectives;
❑ a balance of different types of activity and teaching throughout the week;
❑ differentiation;
❑ appropriate pace;
❑ feedback for pupils;
❑ opportunities for assessment;
❑ monitoring, evaluation and possible modification to medium-term plans.

The purpose of such planning is to enable effective teaching and inform future planning for the whole class, group and individual. It will ensure that the overall curriculum is broken down into smaller units and presented in a meaningful context which combines effective teaching and learning with flexibility.

the teaching and learning that take place. It is also important that there is a whole school curriculum policy which everyone has a part in designing, together with a hierarchy of planning that includes long-, medium- and short-term plans which are all interdependent on each other and are followed and used by all teachers. In fact, a curriculum that is developed in order to move the school forward successfully can be summarised as follows:

❑ It has implications for the educational experiences of all children.
❑ It is important for the quality of teaching and learning.
❑ Following the curriculum will lead to school improvement.
❑ In order to use the curriculum, colleagues will have to use their own initiative, knowledge and ideas.

4

TARGET SETTING AND RAISING ACHIEVEMENT

This chapter looks at:

❑ collecting information;
❑ the first steps towards target setting;
❑ the advantages and disadvantages of target setting;
❑ the purpose of target setting;
❑ forecasting and setting targets;
❑ the cycle of raising attainment;
❑ planning to raise achievement;
❑ removing some of the barriers to raising pupil achievement.

It considers the importance of setting targets to raise attainment and the ways in which school leaders can improve this process.

INTRODUCTION

All schools have to set targets for the end of Key Stage scores in English, Maths and Science. This owes a lot to the fact that the Secretary of State for Education has raising standards as one of his central educational aims. His key date is 2002 and the national targets for this year are that at the end of Key Stage 2, 80 per cent of children will achieve level 4 and above in English and 75 per cent will achieve level 4 and above in Maths. Setting targets, however, will not make these scores happen. Just saying to teachers that a certain percentage will achieve certain goals will not make those goals more attainable. Target setting is really about knowing what your children are capable of, having high expectations and knowing what needs to happen in order to satisfy those expectations.

The DfEE (1996) publication, *Setting Targets to Raise Standards: A Survey of Good Practice* suggests that: 'Schools should monitor their performance regularly with the aim of identifying and taking specific action to raise standards of achievement. They should set clear targets, appropriate to their own circumstances and build them into any post inspection action plan and school development plan' (1996: 7)

This statement places target setting at the centre of how to raise achievement and makes it quite clear that as a process, target setting happens after all the information about ability and attainment has been collected.

COLLECTING INFORMATION

Assessment

The material on assessment that can be available could include:

❑ baseline assessment on entry to school in the Reception class;
❑ national tests at 7 and 11;
❑ SEN information through an Individual Education Plan (IEP);
❑ QCA tests in English and Maths;
❑ teacher assessments;
❑ other tests, including reading tests and spelling profiles;
❑ computer profiling systems such as COPS.

Using the evidence gathered from such assessments will mean that predicting achievement should be much more accurate and that more realistic targets can be set for both individual pupils and for year groups. School improvement and raising achievement can also be measured against the achievements of other schools, because the statistics are available throughout LEAS and are there to be used as tools for raising standards.

When looking at statistics that give the scores of your school as well as those for other schools both locally and nationally and with comparable numbers of SEN children and free meals, you will find that some perform better than other similar ones. Yours might be better or worse than others. If this is the case, it is important to ask certain questions which include:

❑ Why is it that some schools like ours can achieve results which appear to be much better?
❑ What are they doing that we can learn from?

❏ What do we have to do to achieve similar results?
❏ How can we plan such progress and over what period of time?

If we agree that all schools have similar collections of data that make it possible to make comparisons, then there are several key questions which the analysis of all the assessment data available might help teachers to answer. Table 4.1 suggests what those questions are.

Table 4.1 *Questioning the school data*

❏ How is our school currently performing in English, Maths and Science?
❏ Are some classes in the school more effective than others?
❏ Are some parts of individual subjects better or worse than others, eg Reading within English at Key Stage 1?
❏ Are some groups of pupils doing better than others, for example boys in Maths, girls in writing or different ethnic groups?
❏ How do the achievements in the subject compare with previous years?
❏ How does the school's performance compare with other local schools, the whole LEA and nationally?

THE FIRST STEPS TOWARDS TARGET SETTING

Obviously, this kind of monitoring of test results and other data is only worthwhile if everyone understands why it is being done and it is used in some way to make genuine improvements.

No one can raise achievements alone and no one should be expected to take on the sole responsibility for setting any kind of attainment target. It must be a joint effort with time set aside to discuss achievement and progress and, at the same time, to look closely at the levels of attainment of all the teaching groups in the school.

The first step towards target setting is to use the 'target-setting pro forma'. It is quite a simple form and if it is completed as a group effort using all the teachers who are involved with a particular group or class of children, it will allow you to calculate target percentages in each of the three core subjects.

1. Children who will achieve level 2+/4+

2. Children who should reach level 2+/4+

3. Children who could reach level 2+/4+ with support

4. Children who might reach level 2+/4+ with a lot of support

5. Children who will not reach level 2+/4+ but will need SEN support

Figure 4.1 *Target-setting pro forma*

Using the target-setting pro forma

The actual pro forma has five boxes and looks as shown in Figure 4.1. It is better to have a separate form for each Key Stage. For simplicity, this example combines Key Stages 1 and 2. There are further examples of target setting in this way in Smith (2000) *Improving Pupil Achievement Through Target Setting* and Smith (2001) *Raising Attainment in the Primary School* .

The name of each child in the class needs entering on the form using the advice and expertise of all those teachers who have worked with the children and all the assessment data that is available.

Box 1 and Box 2

It is relatively easy to identify those children who, barring a sudden problem, will achieve the appropriate levels of 2+ at Key Stage 1 and 4 + at Key stage 2. If you want to, and this would be useful, you could also decide who should achieve levels 3 and 5, but this pro forma is really about being able to find the basic percentage figures for levels 2+ and 4+. So, the first thing to do is to put the names of all the children whom you feel confident about in Box 1 and those whom you are less confident about, but whom you have no real misgivings about, in Box 2.

Box 3 and Box 4

These are the difficult ones where discussion is essential. This is also the area where effective schools will set realistic, achievable but difficult targets because they know that what they teach and how they do it will have an effect. They will also be schools that are confident in their abilities and who have high expectations.

In Box 3 place the children who 'could' reach level 2+ and 4+ with support and in Box 4, those who 'might' do the same. Obviously, those who might are less likely to reach the appropriate level than those in Box 3.

Box 5

The school SEN register should also identify those children whose needs are such that they will be unable to reach level 2+ or 4+ whatever support is available. These children will be at various stages on the SEN register and should be receiving specialist support.

Calculating the percentage

If there are lots of names in Boxes 3 and 4, you have a problem and you will have difficult choices to make, because some of them will achieve the appropriate level and others won't. You have to decide how many. Your knowledge of what has happened in the past with similar children and similar support and what the current children are capable of achieving is crucial. Equally important, however, is how much support you will be able to give them. If you can organise effective booster classes, more progress will be made. If you have good teaching assistants who can work with small groups, then the children are more likely to learn more. You have to decide how many children in these two boxes will reach levels 2+ and 4+.

All you need to do now is add up the number of children in Boxes 1 and 2, and those identified in Boxes 3 and 4, and from this figure you will be able to calculate the target percentage who will achieve the magic levels of 2+ or 4+. The form will also help you identify individual children who need support and where to concentrate that support.

Using the form will also mean that you and your colleagues are concentrating and focusing on pupil performance and by doing this you will be able to remind yourself of the priorities for pupil achievement and what particular cohorts need to achieve.

THE ADVANTAGES AND DISADVANTAGES OF TARGET SETTING

Target setting has a vital part to play in raising achievement but there are both advantages and disadvantages.

Advantages include:

❑ It helps to raise teacher's expectations.
❑ It helps to focus on the potential of individual pupils in a range of areas.
❑ It forces teachers to identify ways to support individual potential.
❑ It sharpens the focus of teachers on whether their teaching is of an appropriate quality.
❑ It allows teachers to examine the relevance and usefulness of their long-, medium- and short-term planning.
❑ It improves pupils' responsibility for their own learning through discussion of specific targets with individual children and by explaining the target-setting process.
❑ It focuses pupils' attention on how they can improve their learning.

Disadvantages include:

❑ Teachers are beginning to give the impression to children and their parents that tests and the test subjects are all that matters.
❑ There is an over-emphasis on target setting in the core subjects.
❑ National tests may reduce the importance and value of knowledge, skills and understanding across the broad swathe of the primary curriculum.
❑ Teachers may unduly focus their knowledge and energy on borderline children (see target-setting pro forma, p 88) to meet a specific target so that can they can prove that they have raised achievement in some measurable way.
❑ Concentrating on 'borderline' children (in spring 1999 the government started its policy of providing 'booster' money for Year 6 children, who with help might achieve level 4 in the national tests) might diminish the need to make sure that all pupils should be enabled to meet their potential.

THE PURPOSE OF TARGET SETTING

The main purpose of target setting has to be to raise achievement. Individual pupils remain at the centre of the process and this means that raising the attainment of each individual pupil will begin to raise the overall achievement of the school. The basic process and purpose of target setting will follow a similar pattern to that in Table 4.2.

Table 4.2 *The purpose of target setting*

Firstly, targets should:
❏   be   Smart
          Measurable
          Appropriate and agreed
          Realistic and recorded
          Time related
❏   take into account the context within which the school and its pupils are working
❏   fit into a cycle of school improvement which involves five stages:

1.   Analysing current performance
2.   Comparing results with other schools
3.   Setting the actual targets
4.   Planning the action
5.   Taking action and reviewing progress

FORECASTING AND SETTING TARGETS

The starting point for any realistic and effective target-setting process is the current attainment of individual pupils. Improving performance from that beginning needs to be planned and should, if it is successful, not only raise individual performance but extend the improvements across a wider range of children.

Such a plan must involve:

❏   concerted and rigorous effort;
❏   a focus on improving classroom practice;
❏   the appropriate use of all available resources.

Table 4.3 *The target-forecasting process*

---

1. The individual child
Each teacher needs to use current assessment material and any other available data, including each child's attitude and rate of progress, in order to forecast what level he or she is likely to achieve at the end of the next Key Stage. Each teacher must also consider what the pupil could achieve if a real challenge were added, or if, for example, more support or more one-to-one teaching were provided.

2. Making comparisons
Forecasts and potential targets need to be discussed across the age ranges and with previous teachers. This wider internal perspective needs to be matched against the performance of schools with similar cohorts to ensure that the school is setting its sights high enough.

3. Wide discussions
Draft targets need to be discussed with governors and the LEA before they are finalised. While it is the governors who are required to set targets, it is the school and the teachers who will base their decisions on their understanding of the current attainment of the pupils in the cohort being considered and on what would be challenging for those pupils.

4. Annual target reviews
During any year pupils may make more or less progress than expected. It is important to review targets each year alongside the next set of assessment data that becomes available. Doing this will help the targets to be both realistic and challenging.

The forecasting process will follow the pattern as suggested in Table 4.3.

THE CYCLE OF RAISING ATTAINMENT

If target setting is used effectively it will mean that all the different aspects of a pupil's performance are put at the centre of the school's work. A structured way to represent this is to use a circular planning model, which suggests that the process is continuous rather than having a specific

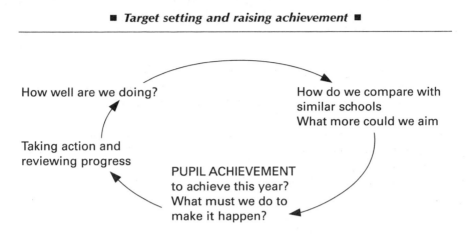

Figure 4.2 *The target-setting cycle*

beginning and a definite and finite end. In fact, rather than looking for and expecting an end to the process, it is far better and more appropriate to expect a continuous pattern of development as illustrated in Figure 4.2. This will begin with the question of 'How well are we doing?'

Looking at the five stages in the process in more detail and asking key questions will make it possible to suggest the ways in which target setting is a whole-school issue. It will also be possible to identify various roles for different colleagues in the struggle to raise pupil achievement.

How well are we doing?

❑ Teachers must be able to show that they have achievement data on each pupil in their class, so that they can analyse his or her performance.
❑ Subject coordinators have to monitor and evaluate their individual subject throughout the school.
❑ The headteacher and senior teachers should understand and be able to analyse broad trends that are related to the progress of individuals and classes.
❑ Teachers should use open evenings and any other relevant opportunities to discuss how individual pupils are performing, with their parents.
❑ Governors should have enough information to be able to ask challenging questions about the school's performance in measurable tests.

How well should we be doing?

❑ Class teachers should be able to set specific targets for each individual child in their class and review them against previous targets and previous knowledge of their ability.

❏ Subject coordinators have to be able to analyse the performance of year groups and classes against their knowledge of previous and/or similar groups.

❏ The headteacher and senior managers must be in a position to compare current and previous results against those from similar schools.

❏ Information given to governors should allow them to understand how the school's performance in measurable tests compares with schools locally and nationally.

What should we aim to achieve this year?

❏ Teachers must have high expectations of all their pupils and be involved in and support the target-setting process.

❏ Subject coordinators should be in a position to be able to help class teachers forecast achievement in their subject.

❏ Both the headteacher and all senior teachers must be able to set realistic and challenging targets for improvement.

❏ Parents should be helped to understand what their child's targets are and, where appropriate, the kinds of support that is available to secure his or her achievement.

❏ The governors have to be presented with all the target-setting evidence that is available so that they are able to agree the targets that the school intends setting.

What must we do to make this happen?

❏ Children need to be told what their targets are and shown how to achieve them in small, structured steps.

❏ Each teacher has to plan in a structured way the action that they need to take in order to improve individual pupil performance.

❏ Coordinators of individual subjects need to know what action class teachers are taking so that they can be in a position to offer expert advice.

❏ All teachers need to see that the headteacher and senior management are taking action and are determined to raise attainment.

❏ The governors must have an overview of the plans that are in place to meet the targets.

Taking action and reviewing progress

❑ The school and classroom environment encourages children to maintain positive attitudes and to work hard.

❑ All agreed plans, curriculum plans, action plans that have been developed to raise achievement and to meet targets must be implemented by all teachers.

❑ Coordinators need to work alongside teachers to support target setting and to help raise achievement.

❑ The headteacher and senior teachers must continue to monitor and evaluate the actions that are taken to improve pupil performance.

❑ The governing body should continue to check that targets are properly monitored and reviewed.

This section of the chapter should have identified the importance of target setting and, at the same time, made it clear that target setting will not, on its own, raise the achievement of individuals or classes or year groups. Individual teachers and coordinators have to have action plans within the overall umbrella of strategies agreed by senior teachers and governors. In earlier chapters, a whole school ethos has been discussed and it is important yet again not to underestimate the power and effectiveness of groups, teams and the whole school working together. Individual teachers cannot work alone. Target setting will be much more effective if there is a whole school approach where decisions can be taken on:

❑ how the school is organised;
❑ what effective teaching actually is;
❑ what is the most effective way to organise the curriculum;
❑ the success of the planning process;
❑ how teams of teachers can help raise achievement;
❑ the important role of subject coordinators, senior teachers and the headteacher.

PLANNING TO RAISE ACHIEVEMENT

There are four main strategies for raising achievement. They are:

1. a planned curriculum that has both breadth and depth;
2. schemes of work that break down the curriculum into manageable chunks;

3. effective lesson plans;
4. differentiation, so that each child is able to work to his or her own potential and not perform tasks that are either too easy or too difficult.

Long-, short- and medium-term planning together with the basic outline of a planned curriculum have already been discussed in Chapter 3. There are some other specific issues that will need addressing here, but this section will concentrate more on schemes of work and differentiation.

1. A planned curriculum

First of all, let's look briefly at the key components of the end product of successful planning, which is what actually happens in the classroom. Basically this will mean that each teacher is able to answer the following questions:

❏ What is the purpose of my teaching?
❏ What will the children actually do to achieve these purposes?
❏ What resources do I need to allow these activities to happen?
❏ What outcomes in terms of completed work will be produced as a result of these activities?
❏ How can I assess whether my teaching has been successful?
❏ Will the work I have planned fit into the time that the long-term planning agrees is available?

Planning is vitally important but the results of the planning need to be reflected in manageable chunks of work. It may be the case, in your school, that the long-term plan with its broad curriculum map, the medium-term plan with its breakdown of work in term or half-term chunks and the short-term weekly and daily planning are sufficient to identify all the important and manageable sections of the curriculum. QCA are producing all kinds of schemes of work, as are many local authorities, and it is also true to say that OFSTED like to see schemes of work as an integral part of school planning. You may disagree and feel that this is just another layer of paperwork that you could well do without.

2. Schemes of work

This is what is to be taught and it is useful in that it can provide a summary of what has to be covered in each subject. Each scheme of work needs to show progression in terms of content from year to year, and in order to be effective it will also need to be able to:

❑ provide a framework within which to work;
❑ help to promote continuity and progression;
❑ give confidence and create teacher security;
❑ help measure success or failure in terms of what is being taught within the agreed curriculum;
❑ confirm to staff what it is that they should actually be teaching.

QCA schemes of work can be used as they are or can be modified to suit the specific needs of individual schools. It is important to have a coherent plan in which the details of teaching and learning can be easily translated into classroom practice, because knowing what is to be taught, how it is to be taught and when it is to be taught is one of the keys to raising standards and improving pupil achievement. It is also important to make sure that teachers are given an opportunity, within a not too prescriptive scheme of work, to convert what they have into their own creative classroom practice. Doing this will mean that they are able to retain confidence in their own abilities. Despite these provisos, Table 4.4 suggests what should be included in a successful scheme of work.

Table 4.4 *Schemes of work*

The following should be included in your scheme of work:

❑ record-keeping procedures;
❑ assessment and evaluation procedures, including examples of children's work to indicate development and levels of attainment;
❑ links to other curriculum areas where this is appropriate;
❑ links with commercial schemes;
❑ resources to be used including computer software;
❑ recommended books for teachers to use;
❑ list of TV programmes and available videos;
❑ suggestions for displays;
❑ content guideline including an indication of the main knowledge, concepts, skills and attitudes to be addresses in each year;
❑ an approximate amount of time to be allocated each week;
❑ suggested differentiated work for able and less able children.

3. Lesson plans

As with short-term planning, the scheme of work, no matter how detailed, has to be broken down into lessons occupying a fixed amount of class teaching time. These need to be accessible, simple and easily understood. It is also important that they can be referred to quickly, as a reminder for the teacher who wrote them, as well as being a source of information and continuity that will enable other teachers who might take the class to teach to the same curriculum using the same content. This will reduce uncertainty to a reasonable level and increase the probability of children being provided with an appropriate level of high quality teaching.

Lesson planning, which is the short-term part of the planning process, takes time and it is true to say that many teachers are expressing concerns about the amount of time it takes. This is a valid argument and it will continue to be worrying for as long as the curriculum is demanding and complex. The problem can only be reduced if teachers find it possible to devote a minimum amount of time to maximum effect so that the educational needs of all the children are met.

It is impossible to suggest a definitive method of writing short-term plans in terms of what is going to happen in each lesson. All schools will have plans that are similar, but equally all schools will have significant differences in how they produce short-term plans. It is possible, however, to suggest certain areas of knowledge that have to be covered. Figure 4.3 does this and, in understanding each section, it is important to see it as the equivalent of climbing stairs towards a higher standard.

4. Differentiation

Teachers must differentiate their teaching to cater for the varied and complex needs of all the children in their class. This basically means setting tasks that meet the needs of all the children, and there are several strategies that can be used. These will include:

❑ setting a task and allowing different children longer to complete it;
❑ setting a task but changing the instructions and vocabulary that is used for different children;
❑ allowing children to respond in different ways and at different levels to a task;
❑ asking different levels of questions of different children;
❑ using different criteria to measure success;
❑ accepting different outcomes for the same task depending on ability;

STEP 6: Evaluating knowledge The child is able to take decisions and make judgements that are based on evaluating the knowledge and information he or she has available.
STEP 5: Synthesising knowledge and information The child is able to form new relationships and combine knowledge and information from different areas to create new blocks of understanding.
STEP 4: Analysing knowledge The child has the ability to divide blocks of knowledge and information into parts and to create new relationships between the different sections.
STEP 3: Applying knowledge The child is able to apply the knowledge and information learnt in a variety of situations that differ from the original learning context.
STEP 2: Understanding the knowledge The child is able to interpret, translate and summarise information.
STEP 1: Knowledge Each child is able to recognise, learn and recall information.

Figure 4.3 *Levels of learning*

❏ using different resources;
❏ offering different levels of support.

All the strategies can be used in any primary classroom, but at the same time, there seem to be two basic techniques for differentiation that are the most common (there are others which will be mentioned briefly later in the chapter): 1)differentiation by task, which means that there are different levels of tasks set, some of which are easier and some more difficult; 2) differentiation by outcome – a whole class task is set but different outcomes are expected from children with different levels of ability.

Differentiation by task

If tasks are set that are achievable, children will be stimulated to achieve more because they will be able to recognise their own successes. To do this is not easy, because the tasks that are set have to be matched precisely to the ability levels of the group. This will mean a common thread to the lesson and different tasks set for different ability levels. At the same time, it is important not to have too many different groups working on separate tasks within the classroom.

The literacy hour and the numeracy strategy have got it right by making it clear that four groups are the maximum that can be taught effectively by one teacher and that three is probably more easily managed. Even with this ideal number of differentiated groups, teaching is not easy. If the tasks that are set are too easy, the children will not be given the opportunities to demonstrate skills of which they are capable. On the other hand, if tasks are set that are too difficult, self-esteem will be lowered, confidence will be undermined and the teacher may have to spend a lot of time with individual children or specific groups who should really be able to work with little teacher input.

For successful teachers, differentiation is the integral part of each day's lessons. This will mean a considerable amount of preparation if the tasks are to be set accurately for different ability levels. The use of differentiation as a strategy is based on a deep understanding of each child's individual needs and abilities, and mustn't be so rigidly applied as to make it difficult for pupils to change between ability groups.

Differentiation by outcome

Setting a task for the whole class and expecting different outcomes has many advantages and few disadvantages. Every child will be able to recognise that if the same work is set for everyone they are all being treated equally. This will also mean that if it is appropriate they will all be able to support each other in the task that has been set. At the same time, each child will be able to show what he or she can do and there will be plenty of time for each child to show positive achievement. This kind of whole class task, however, will frequently have to be open ended and some children find this kind of activity more difficult than more straightforward activities that require more straightforward answers.

For teachers, setting the same kind of tasks and expecting different outcomes makes it easier to differentiate between the various levels of attainment. It is also easier to mark work that is set in this way and to organise teaching and learning resources. At the beginning of the lesson when the same task is introduced to the class, there are good opportunities for whole class discussions and well-structured questions that can be targeted at different levels for different pupils. Obviously, there are some drawbacks and areas of strengths and weakness in both methods, but a combination of the two styles is an excellent strategy for raising achievement and improving performance.

Differentiated lesson plans

Lesson plans and differentiated short-term planning have to reflect opportunities for differentiation. Some of the criteria that will help in this will include the following:

❏ setting clear lesson objectives;
❏ structuring the lesson into blocks of time for different activities, eg introductory, main activity, plenary;
❏ using appropriate teaching styles for different activities, eg whole class, small group and individuals;
❏ setting clear and achievable goals;
❏ differentiating between three or four groups;
❏ deciding the kinds of questions that are going to be asked;
❏ planning homework that will extend the work that is done in the class;
❏ indicating how the lesson will link into other lessons.

Detailed schemes of work and thorough lesson planning will not raise standards without differentiation. This is a difficult challenge, because ensuring rigour, pace and challenge for able pupils while at the same time making sure that low achievers understand and complete work is not easy. Most primary teachers with up to 30 children in their classes find matching the level of the work set to the level of ability of the children difficult, and what needs rejecting completely is the idea that it is possible to teach every child separately. This is impossible, but at the same time it is important to recognise the existence of different ability levels. Montgomery (1989) suggested that there were three further ways of modifying teaching techniques to achieve successful differentiation. They were:

1. differentiation by giving more time;
2. differentiation by content level;
3. differentiation by personal contribution.

All three can be considered alongside the two earlier strategies of differentiation which were either by outcome or by task.

Differentiation by giving more time

If your teaching is aimed towards the middle of the ability range, those children who are less able may well experience difficulties and lose both motivation and self-esteem. Effective teachers will give such children more time to complete tasks and more teacher time to discuss how to complete the work that has been set. This is not as easy as it may seem, because other children, especially the more able, will receive less time with the teacher and, by completing tasks more quickly, may present organisational and classroom management problems.

Differentiation by content level

This is really streaming by ability within a single class or group of children. It means that it minimises the problems that children will have with the material as well as allowing the teacher to spend time equally among children of different abilities, because the tasks that are set are geared to the children's individual needs and abilities. The children will know who has easier work and whose work is more difficult. They may equate lower-level work with lower status. If this happens, it may mean that this strategy of differentiation is divisive. If this is the case then to make it successful the teacher must make it very clear to all children that they are all valued equally.

Differentiation by personal contribution

This is a complex method of differentiation which demands considerable organisational and classroom management skills. It works like this. All the children in the class are set the same task, but the manner in which it is set, the strategies used for its completion and the acceptance of different outcomes mean that individuals are able to work at their own level. There is a reliance on individual and group strategies and a cooperative atmosphere in the classroom is essential. When it is used well it can avoid social divisions and overcome any kind of attention seeking and disruption because of frustration caused by too easy or too difficult work. It is also possible that by using this strategy all pupils will feel some kind of ownership of both the curriculum content and the processes they are going through.

It is important to repeat that delivering an effective curriculum is not possible without differentiation. It is a difficult balancing act, but every teacher has to match work to ability so that all children are working at a level that they can cope with and at a level that helps them progress, raises their attainment and helps the school improve.

Table 4.5 is the final section in this chapter and it raises 10 further issues related to differentiation. By taking them into account it should be possible to use some or all of them to raise attainment and improve learning.

REMOVING SOME OF THE BARRIERS TO RAISING PUPIL ACHIEVEMENT

Despite target setting, supportive teaching, a positive whole school ethos and differentiation in the classroom, some children will fail in some areas of the curriculum. Some of the reasons for this to happen include the following:

❑ poor behaviour and an inability to follow rules;
❑ low self-esteem;
❑ poor attendance;
❑ special educational needs;
❑ poor socialisation skills in the whole of the family which will limit productive contact with the home;
❑ lack of parental support;
❑ lack of participation in extra-curricular activities;
❑ family circumstances such as divorce, etc.

This is a formidable list of problems, many of which are unexpected in the sense that the reasons for them are not always known by the school and are not always easy to observe. The school can help resolve some of them by its positive actions and by its ability to draw in other agencies such as social services and educational psychologists.

Self-esteem is critical, and raising and improving a child's self-perception as well as resolving other issues such as poor attendance will go a long way towards raising individual achievement.

Known reasons for low achievement

These are the more predictable and more easily observed reasons that so obviously limit the achievements of individual children. In one sense, they are many of the 'unexpected' factors manifesting themselves as 'known' classroom behaviours. They will include:

❑ being slow to settle in to begin tasks;
❑ routinely copying other children's work;

Table 4.5 *Further issues related to differentiation*

1.	Be realistic . . . how much differentiation is possible and manageable?	Teaching to three levels, higher, average and low attainers, is not perfect but it is achievable.
2.	Decide whether to differentiate by activity or outcome.	If you are using three groups, differentiation by activity should be possible and effective. It will mean that concepts can be discussed as a class and then tasks will be tailored to the needs of the three groups. This is the way that the numeracy and literacy strategies are organised, although they suggest four groups or more, which can be unmanageable.
3.	Assess the children in your class in a differentiated way.	Make the assessment tasks fit the needs and abilities of your differentiated groups. This will make more work for the teacher but makes for a more effective system of assessments for the children.
4.	Differentiate by using different groupings for different subjects.	Children who are in the lower group for numeracy may not be low attainers in literacy. Some children, however, may well be in the same group for all subjects, so it is not always possible to change groups. Where it is possible, it will allow you to cater more successfully for individual needs.
5.	Change groupings when and where necessary.	Children learn at different speeds and some children find learning difficult because of their behaviour. These are both good reasons for having a flexible

	attitude to teaching groups and understanding how important it is to change them when it becomes necessary.
6. Make sure that the differentiated tasks are challenging.	The teaching groups that have been created should mean that all the children's learning needs are met. It is important to make sure that the tasks they are set and asked to complete meet their learning needs.
7. Check that lack of specific skills isn't holding children back.	A lack of basic skills in one area, eg poor pencil control or poor spelling, should not be seen as a lack of ability in other areas of the curriculum.
8. Understand why certain children are in certain groups.	It is important that you know why you have grouped your class in the way you have. A basic question that needs to be asked is: 'What criteria do you use and is it flexible enough to cater for the needs of individual children?'
9. Differentiate in whole class sessions.	This plays its part in the numeracy strategy and is illustrated in the training materials. It means that it is important to ask differentiated questions so that every child can feel that he or she has taken part in the lesson.
10. Differentiate the support you offer.	With three differentiated teaching groups in the classroom it is possible over a period of a week to give support to each group and individual children for an appropriate amount of time.

❏ distracting other children;
❏ being easily distracted;
❏ inability to complete homework to deadlines;
❏ talking rather than listening;
❏ poor response to praise;
❏ working to a superficial level.

Most, if not all of these barriers to learning can be exacerbated by how the school functions and responds but, unless it is a recognised SEN issue, all of the reasons are caused by the home, parents and family. The seeds of failure are already established before the child starts school and, where possible, it is essential to educate parents in how to work with their children at home. Failing to change parental attitudes will fail the child.

Attitudes to learning

Attitudes to school, to adults, including teachers, and to authority in the form of rules and ways of working in classrooms can be more powerful as a reason for low attainment than any innate ability or measurable intelligence.

Children who behave well, relate to their peers and to adults and are interested and able to sustain concentration by being involved in the tasks set will learn and achieve. If the opposite is true and if a child has negative attitudes, low attainment is more likely to be the norm. Some of the negative attitudes that have to be overcome in order to raise achievement will include:

❏ difficulty in participating in cooperative group work;
❏ refusal to join in discussions;
❏ unwillingness to persevere with tasks;
❏ lack of enthusiasm;
❏ lack of pride in their work;
❏ inability to share resources;
❏ hatred of making mistakes and an inability to learn from them;
❏ inability to work without the direct supervision of an adult.

Earlier chapters have suggested the kinds of positive approaches such as whole school ethos and the design of the curriculum that will help support children who are unwilling and unable to learn. Chapter 5 will develop strategies for managing what happens in the classroom in order to overcome low achievement. It is important to remember, however, that such factors as low self-esteem and poor attitudes to learning present teachers with considerable barriers to raising achievement in their classrooms. Effective teaching, which is the subject of the next chapter, will play a leading role in breaking down barriers to learning.

IMPORTANT POINTS

❏ The starting point in the process of setting targets to raise achievement is the collection and analysis of data. This will mean using all the data that is available, which will include the teacher's own levels of achievement for each child, national test scores, QCA scores and any other data that is available nationally and locally. Collecting this data is only the starting point and it has to be analysed in a way that will create a level of attainment for each child and, when collected together, for the whole cohort or year group.

❏ After this starting point there is a cycle of raising achievement which begins with target setting and goes on to ask wider, relevant questions about classes or year groups. These include making sure that you actually know how well the school is doing from your analysis, and asking the question, 'How well should we be doing?' This will involve widening the data collection to that of other similar schools. Collecting data and setting targets is relatively simple. What happens in classrooms will determine whether it is successful there were short sections in this chapter suggesting what needs to happen in order to meet the targets that have been set. Schemes of work and lesson plans are important (short-term planning was discussed in Chapter 3), as is differentiation in the classroom and those teaching and classroom management skills which recognise barriers to raising attainment and are able to do something about it. This is the subject of Chapter 5.

SUCCESSFUL TEACHING AND EFFECTIVE CLASSROOM MANAGEMENT

This chapter looks at:

❑ effective and ineffective teaching;
❑ positive classrooms;
❑ the all-seeing teacher;
❑ lesson structure;
❑ classroom relationships between teacher and taught;
❑ assertive teaching;
❑ professional skills;
❑ why are discipline and effective control important?

It considers the importance of effective teaching and the ways in which school leaders can improve their performance.

INTRODUCTION

Let's start this chapter by trying to recognise the broad differences between an effective and an ineffective teacher. This is important, because managing and controlling what happens in individual classrooms is vital to the success of the whole school. Teachers often view themselves and their skills in a negative light and it is a commonly held view that the skills that are necessary to teach well are natural and vocational gifts that you either do or do not possess. While this may be true of a small minority, it can be damaging to those teachers who are experiencing crises of confidence and are laying the blame on their own inadequacies rather than on the lack of particular skills, many of which can be learnt. All teachers have a fund of skills, expertise and knowledge, and developing these talents and thinking about which of them work best will not only help improve the skills, but will also develop new ones in a focused way.

The *Chief Inspector's Annual Report* (OFSTED, 1995) comments on high standards of achievement in the following way: 'The largest single factor contributing to this generally healthy position is the quality of the teaching' (1995: 1). Thinking about which skills and strategies will work best, why they work and in what circumstances will lead to more effective teaching. Having emphasised this kind of thoughtful approach, it is important to realise that very skilled teachers make classroom management look easy, and each individual teacher needs to be able to choose from available options. This is a very important process because, as we all know, teachers are more likely to have well-managed classrooms if they are skilled at providing purposeful and stimulating learning experiences to all their pupils by using a variety of delivery methods and styles.

What happens in classrooms is complex, and while OFSTED inspections will provide a useful list of criteria which will help define what they see as good teaching, it should not be expected to stand alone as a definition of good practice (see Chapter 6). The curriculum will suggest the content of what is taught but it will not help us to 'nationalise' the styles and processes necessary to deliver the curriculum. And why should it? Teaching is a creative process rather than a set of prescribed events, and those who do suggest that they can easily define 'good' teaching often appear to think that it is easy to do so and that there is an accepted list of criteria with which everyone agrees. In reality, what is accepted as 'good' and 'bad' teaching can vary widely . . . unless, of course, you want to play safe and work all the time within OFSTED's narrow range of criteria.

EFFECTIVE AND INEFFECTIVE TEACHING

The effective teacher

Smith (1995) begins to define what should happen in an effective classroom when teachers manage the learning processes effectively. There are many other definitions and others will appear later in this chapter, but in this first summary it is suggested that in an effective classroom:

❑ targets and outcomes are built into the teaching;
❑ record keeping is thorough and realistic;
❑ all areas of the curriculum are taught effectively;

❑ children feel good about themselves and are encouraged to have high self-esteem;
❑ there is a work ethic and on-task behaviour;
❑ parents are seen as partners in the learning process;
❑ discipline and control are developed firmly and consistently;
❑ praise is emphasised rather than criticism;
❑ work outcomes are varied and interesting;
❑ teaching styles are varied to suit the content of the curriculum and the needs of the children.

He argues that a class taught by an effective teacher 'would be full of lively, interested and positive children who achieve high standards. There will be low stress and little tension. There will be a lot of group cooperation and tolerance. The children should live up to the teacher's high expectations and behave accordingly . . .' (1994: 105).

The ineffective teacher

In contrast, Smith identifies several criteria which he suggests help identify what he calls a 'bad' teacher. Some of them state that this teacher:

❑ acts as a kind of adult bully;
❑ creates tension based on the pressure of unrealistic goals and deadlines;
❑ emphasises punishment rather than praise, stress rather than calm, and hardly ever smiles or laughs;
❑ has a similar level of punishment for all incidents, big and small;
❑ often stifles enthusiasm and sees lively and curious children as a threat;
❑ frowns on a wide curriculum and sees education in terms of a narrow range of basic skills;
❑ sees outcomes as standard and stereotyped and develops a restrictive timetable that dominates every routine;
❑ defines self-expression, the 'arts' and most forms of spontaneous creativity as not being 'work';
❑ has a suspicious attitude towards change rather than an informed opinion;
❑ demands passive learning and has a single dominating teaching style;
❑ often insults children and yet expects good manners and tolerance.

He goes on to suggest 'that if most of these attributes are present, children will often produce less and of a lower standard because they are working at the pace of the slowest and what they do is teacher controlled. The stress of such a regime might be such that many children become cowed and submissive . . . A teaching style dominated by criticism rather than praise would lead to fear rather than good behaviour' (1994: 106).

Obviously, there are some contentious suggestions in Smith's article which, by being originally published in 1988 and reprinted in 1994, might be seen as somewhat dated. What is true, however, is that whatever definitions and criteria are used, it is essential to minimise 'bad' teaching and maximise 'good' classroom practice.

POSITIVE CLASSROOMS

The Elton Report (1989) was largely ignored and is now forgotten and neglected, which is a great pity as its thorough recommendations recognised many important issues relating to how effective schools function. The report suggests that there is a concept called 'classroom climate' and that teachers who can achieve a positive 'climate' are more successful than those who can't. Teachers who can achieve these positive relationships are described in the following ways:

[They] create a classroom climate in which pupils lose rather than gain popularity with their classmates by causing trouble. They can also spot a disruptive incident in the making, choose an appropriate tactic to deal with it and nip it in the bud. In their relationship with their pupils they always seem to know what is going on behind their backs. Good group managers understand how groups of young people react to each other and to teachers. They also understand and are in full control of their own behaviour. They model the good behaviour they expect from pupils. *All this requires an impressive range of skills.* [my italics]

(1989: 67–68, para 6)

Table 5.1 suggests some of the 'impressive range of skills ' suggested in the Elton Report and, as you read it, compare the similarities and differences between Elton and Smith.

THE ALL-SEEING TEACHER

One of the phrases that has been used already is that of the 'all-seeing teacher'. When effective teachers are teaching a lesson that has been

Table 5.1 *Some teaching skills*

An effective teacher:

❏ knows his or her pupil's names and who their friends are;
❏ can take advantage of unexpected events in the children's lives;
❏ is 'all seeing' and is continually aware of what is happening in the classroom;
❏ plans and organises lessons carefully in order to remain in control and maximise learning opportunities;
❏ arranges the layout of the classroom in order to maximise learning opportunities;
❏ matches work to pupils' abilities (see differentiation, Chapter 4);
❏ paces lessons so that there are no negatively pressurised rushes and no periods of inaction;
❏ models the kind of behaviour that is acceptable;
❏ avoids using group punishments by being capable of finding the right culprit;
❏ is fair and consistent and builds up relationships by reprimanding pupils privately rather than publicly.

planned carefully, they need to be aware of where they are in the classroom and of everything that is happening around them. Good teachers are able to use their eyes productively and to spot trouble in its early stages, ideally before it has had the chance to manifest itself. Not only are they able to use eye contact to express various emotions and feelings, they are also able to sweep the room quickly to take in most if not everything that is taking place in it. The using your eyes diagram in Figure 5.1 is adapted from Smith (1996b). It indicates the areas of the room where the teacher can focus on the children. The biology of the human eye means that there are areas of the classroom where it is difficult, if not impossible, to see what is happening by remaining in the same place. After looking at Figure 5.1 it will be useful to imagine, or even draw a plan of your classroom and think carefully about your responses to the following questions:

❏ Why is it important to move around the classroom?
❏ Whereabouts in your classroom do you have to make sure that you move to?
❏ Are there many 'blind' spots? If there are, what can you do to minimise them?

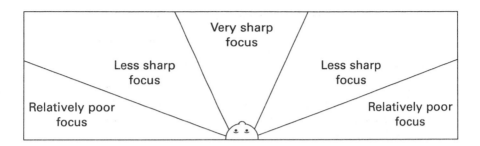

Figure 5.1 *The all-seeing teacher?*

❏ Are you able to talk to the whole class from any position in the room?
❏ Do you need to change any of the furniture round?

Where children are in the classroom

Where children sit and the groups that they work in are very important. You will, after a few days with a class, know who should not sit with whom, and who is capable of working with little supervision. The three most common ways of organising a classroom are:

❏ children working individually;
❏ children working in small groups.
❏ children working as a whole class;

To a large extent, the numeracy strategy and the literacy hour have defined whole class teaching and the activities that individual children are required to do. These individual activities do take place with children sitting in groups, so it is important to organise them for this purpose as well as when you want them to work together cooperatively. Table 5.2 suggests several ways of organising groups of children for different purposes.

Crisis points

It is useful at this point to introduce the concept of crisis points. It is related both directly and indirectly to groups and is an important weapon in the armoury of teaching skills. For example, in both the literacy hour and the numeracy strategy there is movement from whole class to groups to whole class again. In other words, there are specific points in the lesson where activities change and there is physical movement. These can be 'crisis

Table 5.2 *Groups in the classroom*

1. Groups formed for certain tasks: When a teacher decides on a certain piece of work, s/he might have a particular group of pupils in mind who will work cooperatively and collaboratively together, although normally the children may not sit or work together.
2. Specific teaching groups: This is the basic organisation for the literacy hour and the numeracy strategy. Pupils of the same level of ability sit together and work on a common matched task.
3. Pupils who sit together (sometimes called friendship groups): These are usually natural friendship groups where the children normally sit or work
4. Interest groups: These are children who are working in an area of scientific investigation, or on a technology project, and they happen to share the same interests.

points'. If challenging behaviour is going to take place, these are the vulnerable points, and it is important to have well-organised strategies to manage these changes smoothly, quickly and effectively. These crisis points in their widest sense could include:

❑ the time when children are in the classroom before you arrive *(this should never happen)*;
❑ the time pupils are kept waiting for you to start the lesson;
❑ the transition between the teacher stopping the whole-class part of the lesson to children moving to their groups and possibly collecting resources;
❑ the transition between children working on a common group task to working totally on their own;
❑ the return back to whole-class teaching from group or individual work;
❑ the transition between a practical to a silent activity and vice versa;
❑ the effect of a real 'emergency' such as a fire drill, someone fainting or being sick.

LESSON STRUCTURE

Avoiding such crisis points and therefore enabling teachers to teach has to happen. If it doesn't, it will be less easy for the lessons to be effective. There are two basic techniques that need to be used: 1) control and discipline techniques and 2) the actual structure of lessons. Within each technique there are many, many sub-categories and, like most issues in teaching, they are complex because they are about individuals working with large numbers of other individuals who aren't always working to the same script, or having the same agenda. Let's look first at the structure of the lesson, which, of course, has been meticulously planned.

I keep mentioning the literacy and numeracy strategies, and this is because they impose a structure on teachers and define a particular and specific method of classroom organisation which lasts for approximately an hour for each subject. This method of organisation can, if you wish, be applied to other areas of the curriculum. I feel that this will be placing too rigid a structure on the school day and will leave little room for initiative and innovation, as well as limiting 'lessons' to a short period of time when it is sometimes appropriate to have an area of the curriculum, eg Design Technology, lasting for an afternoon. It is interesting to compare my suggested structure, which is based on ideas from the late 1980s, to the literacy and numeracy structures of the late 1990s. There are similarities, which might lead you to think that many teachers had been teaching to a tight structure for many years.

This method is based on an idea in Diane Montgomery's *Managing Behaviour Problems* (1989). I have called it the choreographed lesson plan because it tries to take one step at a time and builds up into a whole timed sequence of events. Table 5.3 lists the five stages in the structure.

Numeracy and literacy have to fall into this kind of neat time span of around an hour. Other lessons do not, and it will be possible to allow a whole afternoon for a themed project or for a science investigation. If this is the case, the choreographed lesson plan can still be used. For example, it could be used twice in an afternoon, that is, in two cycles, or the activity section could be a very long one lasting over an hour. What is important is the combination of whole class teaching and group and individual tasks.

Questions and answers within the lesson structure

In all three methods of teaching, ie literacy, numeracy and the choreographed lesson plan, one of the keys is being able to develop and improve learning through asking questions that can be answered by children of different abilities. There are many reasons why asking the right questions is important. They include:

Table 5.3 *Choreographed lesson plan*

---

1. What the lesson is about: the lesson objectives
There has to be a key issue: a key objective which is related to the National Curriculum programme of studies. Ideally, this should be understood by the children.

2. The introduction
This should last no more than 10 minutes. It should refresh pupils' memories of past lessons and introduce any skills and concepts needed in this lesson. This needs to be a whole class lesson using appropriate questions, which should be differentiated to meet individual needs.

3. First stage (closely linked to second stage) This should be another 10-minute whole class section which goes beyond the introduction and introduces the task using whole class teaching and differentiated questions. If there are different tasks for different abilities, different examples need to be used.

4. Second stage (closely linked to first stage)
This should form the main bulk of the lesson and should, in a total time of one hour, last approximately 20 minutes. It is the activity that should help all the children meet the objective of the lesson. It must be a deliberate activity change to avoid boredom. It could involve group discussion, a group writing activity, individual writing, drawing, reading, note taking, etc. It is important that both teachers and classroom assistants target a particular group of children to work with and that this group rotates each week.

5. Third stage
This lasts about 5–10 minutes and it is the concluding part of the lesson. It is a whole class activity and will be largely dependent on questions and answers. It will require the children to tell themselves and others what they have been doing.

❑ Questions encourage participation and increase pupils' interest and work rate.
❑ They give feedback to the teacher and indicate whether pupils are progressing at an appropriate rate.
❑ They encourage children's reasoning ability.

❑ They test children's knowledge of the subject matter that is being taught.
❑ Targeting questions at particular children can also be part of a teacher's control technique.

Equally as important as asking the right questions is how they are asked. It is no good, for example, asking too many questions in one sequence, or asking questions and demanding answers if they are pitched at too high a level for the majority of the class. It is also important to give children time to answer and then to build on the answers by asking further questions that are designed to increase their knowledge. Some of the questioning techniques that are effective will include:

❑ **Socialising questions** – eg 'Haven't you got a new baby brother this morning . . . ?'
❑ **Questions showing interest in children as individuals** – eg 'That sounds interesting, John. Why not tell everyone about it?'
❑ **Questions that respect individual views** – eg 'What do you think we should be doing to solve this problem?'
❑ **Control questions** – eg 'Why are you doing that?'
❑ **Maintaining control questions** – eg 'Why are you still doing that?'
❑ **Closed questions that ask for basic information and can check known facts** – eg 'Which city is the capital of France?'
❑ **Closed questions that supply an instant solution** – eg 'What is 15 divided by 3?'
❑ **Closed questions that mean that analysis has to take place** – eg 'What is the difference between . . . ?'
❑ **Open-ended questions that explore ideas** – eg 'How do you think they felt . . . ?'
❑ **Open-ended questions that allow comparisons to be made between information and ideas** – eg 'Do you think fox hunting is a good or a bad thing?'
❑ **Open-ended questions that encourage evaluation and decision making** – eg 'Do you think that it is fair to say . . . ?'

Explanations within the lesson structure

Teaching and learning, at its most basic, is about transferring the knowledge that is contained in the curriculum, and much of the work that is completed in the classroom involves improving children's understanding of what it is that is being taught and learnt. The previous short section examined questions and questioning technique. If this is used successfully it will help you explain to the children what they are learning about. It will also be useful in helping them find out what they know or don't know, so that future knowledge and future explanations will be directly related to their attainment. All your teaching skills, including questioning techniques, will be used when you are 'explaining' to your pupils. This is especially true when you consider that you could be explaining in all kinds of different circumstances. For example, explanations will be used in whole class, group and individual teaching sessions; an explanation could be part of classroom control, especially when you are telling a badly behaved child the consequences of his or her actions; or you could be giving precise instructions and asking questions to check understanding about how to perform a specific task.

Table 5.4 looks at six different types of explanations that most teachers will use during any school day. In other words, they are strategies for daily use and, at the same time, they are strategies that help you explain clearly and concisely what it is you are teaching, what your objectives are, what you want your children to learn and what they have to do in order to learn it.

CLASSROOM RELATIONSHIPS BETWEEN TEACHER AND TAUGHT

Earlier in this chapter (p 110) I listed some suggested attributes of bad teaching. They included, among others, such areas as more punishment than praise, setting unrealistic goals, stifling enthusiasm, insulting children and insisting on passive learning. If we are going to teach well and transfer the knowledge of the curriculum effectively, we must make sure that the right relationships exist to enable every pupil to learn. One way, and perhaps the most important way, is to create a positive learning ethos and avoid creating situations where children are unable to reach their full potential because they are afraid of making mistakes and are not encouraged to try and persevere. There are two important ways of describing how teachers work in the classroom:

A **provocative teacher** will provoke difficult relationships and will probably create a narrow teacher-guided environment where little tolerance for the individual is encouraged and punishment rather than praise is the norm. There will be lots of opportunities for on-task working, but because of the nature of the pupil–pupil relationships and teacher–pupil relationships there is a sense that off-task behaviour is preferred by the children. Expectations may well be high but outcomes will be lower and of a predictable sameness.

Table 5.4 *Explaining as a teaching tool*

1. Explaining the classroom organisation and subject procedures
This will include rules and routines and is about giving instructions such as: 'No one runs in the classroom' or 'Everyone puts their hand up to answer questions'. It can also be about stating subject procedures that are absolutes, eg 'Full stops go at the end of sentences' or 'Adjectives describe nouns'.

2. Explaining specific lesson objectives
This is the most appropriate way of starting a lesson. You are stating clearly and concisely what the children should have learnt by the end of the lesson.

3. Explanations of cause and effect
This can be related to specific subjects and in its simplest terms will include examples such as: 'If you subtract 3 from 5 you will have a total of 2.' It can also be linked to a deeper understanding such as: 'The reason why a compass points north is because...' It can also be linked closely to classroom control, and it will include explanations of what will happen to John if he shouts out an answer again and doesn't put his hand up.

4. Explanations about relationships
This is about the links between people, things and events and is a particularly useful technique in Personal, Social and Health Education (PSHE). It could include such explanations as the links between smoking, health and lung cancer; family relationships in sex education; and the link between road deaths and road safety.

5. Explaining concepts
This is very common and the examples are endless. Explanations can vary from the simple fact that salt dissolves in water and sand doesn't, to more complex issues such as magnetism and friction.

6. Explaining processes
This is linked to the relationship between objects or actions and is more about how things work. Again, examples are endless and complex, and will include: how a car engine works; how the blood goes round our bodies; how our pulse and heart rate increase after exercise.

A **supportive teacher** will behave in such a way that pupils and teacher will want to work together. Children will be given the opportunity to grow and develop in a variety of ways and will be encouraged to produce a variety of outcomes in an atmosphere that is firm and consistent but that is also tolerant, with high expectations and a very high proportion of on-task working.

The two lists in Table 5.5 summarise the characteristics of both a provocative and a supportive teacher. It is obvious that effective teachers have more

Table 5.5 *Provocative and supportive teachers*

A provocative teacher:

❏ assumes that pupils don't want to work and, when they don't, assumes that it is impossible to provide the right teaching and learning conditions;
❏ believes that discipline is a confrontation that has to be won;
❏ is unable to defuse situations;
❏ frequently issues unreal ultimatums which lead to more confrontations;
❏ uses inconsistent punishments;
❏ gives preferential treatment to pupils who conform;
❏ always expects deviant pupils to behave badly;
❏ makes negative comments about pupils in public;
❏ avoids as much contact as possible with pupils outside the classroom.

A supportive teacher:

❏ assumes that everyone wants to work and, if they don't, the conditions, rather than the pupils, are at fault;
❏ avoids any kind of favouritism;
❏ avoids confrontation;
❏ hardly ever makes any kind of negative comment about pupils in public;
❏ gives pupils the opportunity to back down and save face when they have to be punished;
❏ assumes that pupils will behave well;
❏ cares about and trusts pupils;
❏ enjoys pupils' company both inside and outside the classroom.

---

than their fair share of 'supportive' characteristics and that being 'provocative' can be added to your list of 'bad' teaching techniques.

ASSERTIVE TEACHING

Assertive teachers are able to establish their authority in the classroom as soon as they walk through the door and they are able to maintain their authority throughout the day. They do this by combining several skills, including how they use their bodies, their voice and their facial expressions.

When you walk into the room, it is important to stand straight with head held high and to use a firm, clear and steady voice at the same time as you maintain eye contact. In other words, you need to behave in such a way that the children in your class know that you are in charge but at the same time, they are not frightened into submission, ridiculed or reduced to having low self-esteem.

An assertive teacher is neither aggressive nor passive. In fact, assertiveness is all about being responsible for your own behaviour by respecting others and being honest. It is about being able to say what you want and feel, but not at the expense of other people. It is also about being self-confident and positive and having the ability to handle conflict by reaching acceptable compromises. Assertiveness assumes that you are able to teach in the following ways:

❏ By **challenging** pupils. This will mean making sure that all the teaching that takes place will bring all children to a point where their chances of success are good.
❏ All children must have the **freedom to make decisions**. They must feel that they have some control over what they learn, how they learn and the pace at which they learn.
❏ There must be **respect** between teacher and pupil and between pupils. This is often developed during the process of establishing classroom rules and making sure that the class teacher is in control.
❏ The teacher is in **control** and the routines and rules must be firm, reasonable and fair.
❏ All children should experience some **success** during each day.

In Table 2.8, there was a suggestion as to how to be assertive with colleagues. I want to look at this is in a slightly different way when teachers are working with children. First of all, let's make sure that we can recognise the difference between assertiveness, aggression and passivity:

1. **Aggressiveness** is about trying to get your own way by making other people feel useless, worthless or small. It doesn't always have to involve conflict, but it usually does by causing verbal or physical hostility.
2. **Passivity** means ignoring your own interests and allowing others to manipulate you. It often means denying your own feelings by not being active or proactive and not recognising that you have needs and goals.
3. **Assertiveness** is all about being responsible for your own behaviour by respecting others and being honest. An assertive person is able to say what they want and feel but not at the expense of other people. It is also about being self-confident and positive and having the ability to handle conflict by reaching acceptable compromises.

Another way of looking at assertive teaching is to recognise some of your basic rights, that is, your rights as a teacher. They are important and include the right to:

❑ be taken seriously;
❑ set your own priorities;
❑ express feelings and opinions;
❑ say no;
❑ make mistakes even when you are trying your hardest;
❑ be in control of your classroom space.

It is also important to be aware of what is effective when explaining the rules of your classroom and the parameters of how you expect your class to behave. How you do this is important, because it is no good expecting children to pick up how to behave and the rules that this involves by a process of osmosis and sheer guesswork. They have to be emphasised, reinforced and repeated over and over again in as assertive a way as possible.

How successful you are at doing this will influence the kinds of relationships you have with your pupils, and this in itself is bound to influence how they learn and their level of attainment. There are several ways to do this but the most common are the following assertive strategies:

1. **Laying down the law** by saying such things as, 'Stand up and wait quietly by the door in single file.'
2. **Explaining** what needs to be done. For example, 'You mustn't point scissors at someone because you might injure them.'
3. **Being indignant**, which could be expressed like this: 'I am really disappointed with your behaviour', or 'That was a really cruel thing to say.'

4. **Making a broad and general statement** such as, 'I'd like to see more good manners this week.'
5. **Being absolutely specific** which may sound like this. 'No one is allowed to shout out. Everyone must put their hand up to answer a question'.
6. Using a **question** to establish a rule, such as, 'Why is it important not to run in the classroom?'
7. **Negotiating rules** is also important. This means knowing what you actually want but allowing the children to suggest it for themselves. An example might be, 'How can we stop so many people moving round the room at the same time?'
8. **Asking rule-specific questions** such as, 'Why is it important not to push when you come into the classroom after break?'

When you are dealing with rules and problems caused by children, the most effective technique is to be assertive and this is something that can be learnt. It involves saying the right things in the right way. As was suggested earlier in the chapter, you will need an upright posture, good eye contact and a firm forceful voice that is not too loud (shouting should not be an option) but is clear and very easy to hear. By being assertive in difficult circumstances, it is possible to improve your feelings about yourself as well as give yourself confidence and prevent yourself from feeling powerless and out of control.

Table 5.6 is a very similar assertive script to Table 2.8. This time, however, it is related to a classroom incident rather than dealing with the relationships between adults. The more times you practise it, the easier it is for you to use the tactics of assertion automatically without having to think about them and without them seeming strained and affected. In other words, practice will mean that they are part of your 'normal' day-to-day strategies for discipline and classroom management.

There are other versions of assertive scripts like this in Rowland and Birkett (1992) and Smith (1996c).

PROFESSIONAL SKILLS

It is a commonly held misconception that individual teachers can deal with any problem that arises, at any time of the day and in any kind of school. This is totally untrue and it is a myth that needs demolishing. There is no such thing as this super teacher who is able to save the world. What teachers have is a range of skills, and many of them, including assertion, have been

Table 5.6 *Assertion in the classroom*

This is a step-by-step guide to what you have to do when you need to be assertive in the classroom. Before reading it, imagine the following scene:

You are having to speak firmly to a child who has been calling other children names and, during the reprimand, he starts shouting at you.

Read the script and then modify it to suit your own needs. The six steps can be used in all kinds of circumstances for all kinds of situations:

1. Summarise whatever caused the problem. Do this simply, calmly and without emotion, eg 'I don't like it when you call other people names and I certainly will not allow anyone to shout at me.'
2. State exactly how you feel . . . remember it is you who is involved, not anyone else, eg 'I am very worried that you have been calling other children names and am very angry that you have shouted at me in that bad tempered way.'
3   Describe as clearly as possible why you feel this way, eg 'First of all, you know that you are expected to be friendly with everyone and I am very concerned that you have called other children names and teased them. Behaving like that is not being friendly and shouting at a teacher makes me very unhappy, because you know that this is against the classroom and school rules.'
4   Sympathise or empathise with the child's point of view, eg 'I am sure that you find some of the children irritating and I am sure that you might feel cross with me sometimes.'
5   Specify exactly what you want to happen in terms of what the child has got to do. It is also important to say what should happen in order to find a solution, a compromise or a way out of the situation, eg 'I want you to stop shouting straight away and I want you to promise me that you will stop calling other people names. If you have got a problem with some of your friends, tell me and I will help you.'
6   Decide what your response will be. It is important that whatever you decide should clarify your position without threatening the child, eg 'If you calm down straight away, you will be able to stay in the classroom and I will talk to you later when you are less bad tempered.'

discussed in this chapter. Some will be rediscovered in the next chapter, which examines OFSTED's model of successful teaching.

What is also true is that certain personal qualities and competencies are useful professional skills, but what is difficult to understand is that such skills may be put under pressure and be unsuccessful in some schools and successful in others. Certain teacher behaviour and use of certain strategies may be seen as successful and an asset in one school and yet seen as creating particular difficulties in another school. Individual differences among teachers' attitudes are also difficult to understand and to learn from. For example, some teachers thrive and enjoy working in schools with a very large proportion of difficult children, whereas this would distress and demoralise equally skilful professionals. One way of trying to understand how different teachers use their professional skills and to help us in understanding this aspect of their jobs is to move towards recognising what it is that teachers do that is effective and raises standards and levels of attainment.

There seem to be three issues, which are included in Table 5.7.

Enjoying the job

One of the main sources of enjoyment for teachers is the positive feedback they receive from children and from colleagues. This mostly happens in well-managed and well-planned classrooms within schools where there is a culture of high standards of work and cooperation. When this kind of feedback does not happen it is usually because children are refusing to cooperate because of their own and their parents' cultural and social inadequacies and/or the teacher's own ineffective use of teaching and classroom management skills. This can lead a teacher to feel a sense of attack on his or her own professionalism and, because teaching is often partly about a projection of individual personality, as an attack on him or her as a person, that is, an attack on what is 'me' or what is 'you'. The effect of this can be lower teacher self-esteem, which can begin a demoralising cycle because low self-esteem will mean that the teacher projects a negative image to the class and this is reflected back by the children, thereby instigating and maintaining a negative cycle which is not particularly conducive to effective teaching. This, of course, is an issue for each individual teacher, but it should not be seen solely as the 'fault' of an individual; it is a whole school issue which will affect how successful the school is.

Of course, when you see that the children you are working with are responding positively your self-esteem is raised and there is a strong feeling of being in control, being positive and being empowered. This in turn will

Table 5.7 *Three areas of professional skills and competence*

---

1. Enjoying the job
Through:
❏ being satisfied with teaching as a career;
❏ being satisfied with how teaching is perceived as a career;
❏ enjoying the positive feedback from colleagues, parents and pupils;
❏ being seen as a valued professional in the school and in the wider society.

2. Being in control
Through:
❏ being responsible for what happens in the classroom;
❏ being partly responsible for what happens in the whole school;
❏ being able to take decisions and influence larger decisions;
❏ knowing that the role in school is important.

3. Being a skilful and competent professional
Through:
❏ feeling that my teaching skills are adequate to the tasks in hand;
❏ being able to start, develop and complete professional duties;
❏ being able to control children and manage the classroom skilfully and successfully;
❏ being in a position to raise standards;
❏ working with other skilful professionals.

---

mean that positive images are projected to each class of children and this sense of the 'positive', which is a kind of feel-good factor, will be projected back from the children, indicating a positive cycle of effectiveness. This suggests a strong case for each teacher to be as skilful a practitioner as possible. It also suggests that this positive cycle needs to be maintained, and if there are children who, by their behaviour, are unable to respond, then serious discussions need to take place around whether to include such children within the mainstream classroom or to exclude them from it.

Figure 5.2 shows the positive and negative cycles and reinforces the power of the effect of being able to teach effectively and enjoy it . . . or to enjoy teaching and do it effectively!

The message is clear and very important. There is a close correlation between negative cycles of behaviour between children and teachers and

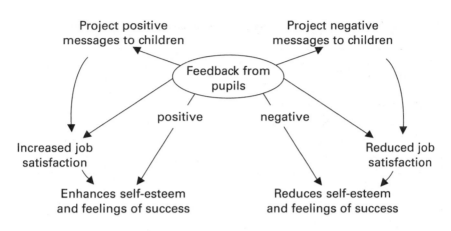

Figure 5.2 *A positive and negative cycle of teaching*

an environment where teaching and learning are not effective. This will mean that children's behaviour will be such that it prevents effective teaching, lessons will be poorly planned and the low expectations will set the scene for a continuous deterioration in relationships, behaviour and learning. As the cycle continues, it will be extremely difficult to stop the wheel turning and reverse the trend. This issue is linked to teacher stress (Chapter 7) and to other areas of this chapter, especially those techniques associated with assertive teaching.

Being in control

I will say it again: no teacher should think that they should shoulder the responsibility for everything that happens in their classroom and in their school. Each classroom is a microcosm of the society outside the school and it will reflect the cultural and intellectual aspirations of the school's 'customers' as well as their attitudes to social behaviour and attitudes. Teachers and schools can and do make a difference and to do this they have to be in control. They have to decide how they want their classroom to function, which will be part of and in agreement with the school's overall ethos, but they don't have to think that they are responsible for what has happened before the lesson and what is likely to happen after it has ended. The more strategies of classroom management that a teacher has, the better their sense of being in control will be; and the more positive their relationships with their children, the more influence they will have before, during and after a lesson.

Being a skilful and competent professional

Teachers are, quite rightly, concerned with their ability to cope with teaching particular classes of children. Without this control, teaching cannot take place. Being unable to control a specific class does not mean that the teacher is professionally incompetent and that the necessary competence cannot be acquired through training or support. In fact it may be the case that specific children are being included in the class and the school at the expense of the education of the majority of those who are well behaved, and that other teachers in the same school would struggle with equal difficulty to control and teach them. Many teachers with reputations for dealing competently with difficult children would find it hard work without the appropriate support and resources.

The most important resource is the individual teacher's resilience, ability to reflect and learn from mistakes, and the power of their own personality, that is, their sense of being themselves. Doubts in professional competence can come largely from trying to treat the act of teaching as a performance rather than developing skills that fit your own individual personality so that it is possible to use them well, all the time.

WHY IS DISCIPLINE AND EFFECTIVE CONTROL IMPORTANT?

It is obvious, and no less important because it is obvious, that without control you cannot use all those skills that transmit and share the knowledge base of the curriculum. It is also important on other, related levels. Rogers in *You Know the Fair Rule* (1991) suggests that **consistent**, **firm** and **fair** teachers will want to use control and discipline to 'lead, guide, direct, manage or confront a student about behaviour that disrupts the rights of others, be they teachers or students', going on to suggest that the aim of discipline is to 'lead a student towards self control and personal accountability' (1991: 10).

There are three reasons for discipline, outlined below.

The conduct of individuals in society

Children have to see the need to respect the rights of others and recognise how their actions affect them. They also need to take responsibility for their own actions and understand the balance between freedom and restriction and tolerance and intolerance. In any school, one of the most important lessons that has to be taught and learnt is how to get on with other children and with adults. This will involve teachers modelling the kind of behaviour that they want. What it shouldn't do is make teachers think that they are failing if what they do does not have an effect on those children who, because of all kinds of inner conflicts, tensions, low self-esteem and anger, do not behave in ways that allow teaching and learning to take place. It is not always the fault of teachers and we should stop them taking this kind of blanket blame for the failings in other areas of society outside the school.

Personal maturity

Most individuals learn more as they mature and develop socially. Teachers need to make sure that children learn and develop the skills associated with:

- ❑ increasing responsibility;
- ❑ tolerance;
- ❑ control of frustration and anger;
- ❑ making more complex social relationships;
- ❑ persevering with the development of their own individual personalities and social skills.

The development of a sense of morality

We all need to be able to recognise what is right and wrong and all those complex behaviour strategies that tell us what is the right and wrong way to behave in different social circumstances. This will involve such issues as:

- ❑ good manners;
- ❑ how to speak to others;
- ❑ how to control destructive emotions such as anger and aggression.

It is also linked to how individual children become aware of the rights of others and move towards a less selfish and more sharing relationships with each other.

To complete this chapter, it is important to consider some general principles that lie behind the achievement of effective discipline and classroom management.

All classroom discipline and control must make sure that it:

❑ emphasises rights, responsibilities and rules;
❑ develops and maintains respect;
❑ follows up all incidents with disruptive children;
❑ includes a wide support base that is there to maintain and improve a positive working atmosphere;
❑ defines who is in authority and the status difference between teachers and children;
❑ is a system that, in disciplining children, gets them back on task as quickly as possible without too long a discussion, without intentional embarrassment and with minimal peer audience involvement;
❑ is part of a whole school working definition of discipline.

IMPORTANT POINTS

❑ This chapter begins by emphasising that there are certain teaching skills that effective teachers use and that by recognising what they are and by teaching in certain ways they create a positive classroom climate where successful teaching and learning can take place. The chapter ends by reintroducing the concept of 'positive teaching'.
❑ This time, however, the emphasis is more on how teachers feel about what they are doing and how they use their professional skills, rather than the skills that are being deployed.
❑ If teachers enjoy their work and feel in charge of what they are doing, there is more chance of positive relationships between teacher and child and, of course, more opportunities for positive and effective learning.
❑ The chapter also recognised that there are styles of teaching and classroom management that equate with a negative approach and negative relationships. These can be overcome by using better planning strategies, more structured lessons and better use of such teaching strategies as questioning and explaining.
❑ Teachers have to be assertive and, like many strategies, this can be learnt. This is very important, because many teachers have crises of confidence if they have difficult classes and/or difficult children in their class.
❑ This means that if they are not as successful as they want to be in changing the behaviour of these children by using what they thought was effective discipline, they become frustrated, with less self-esteem, and this can initiate a downward spiral of stress and negative relationships.

❑ Effective discipline can be learnt, but there are some children who cannot be disciplined and controlled effectively.

❑ Teachers should not take on the blame for these problems and it is important, when such issues arise, that there is a full and intelligent debate about the inclusion of such children in mainstream schools and classrooms.

6

ACCOUNTABILITY AND THE INSPECTION PROCESS

This chapter looks at:

❏ accountability;
❏ performance indicators;
❏ school inspection;
❏ preparing for the inspection;
❏ inspecting your teaching;
❏ other areas of inspection;
❏ after the inspection.

It considers the importance of accountability and the inspection process and the ways in which school leaders can prepare for inspection.

INTRODUCTION

This chapter is about accountability and finding out how effective each school actually is. School inspections are carried out by OFSTED and their reports become public documents. This chapter, however, is also concerned with how individual teachers and schools monitor their own progress.

Early in 1992 the Education (Schools') Act changed the way schools were to be inspected. Her Majesty's Inspectorate was disbanded as the sole department responsible for standards in schools and was replaced by the Office for Standards in Education (OFSTED). Several changes stood out and several changes to the inspection process occurred during the 1990s. Here are some of them:

❏ School inspections are no longer exclusively in the hands of educationalists but involve contracted 'lay' inspectors and the views of parents.

❑ OFSTED would move away from being partly developmental (ie the inspectors suggesting ways in which schools could move forward in the light of the inspection report) to being judgemental, grading teachers and using words such as 'good', 'satisfactory' and 'poor'.
❑ Their judgements would be made public in a written report which would be available to everyone who wanted or needed to read it.
❑ There would be a list of criteria and a formal structure to the inspection process which was designed to ensure uniformity in how the inspection was carried out and what was inspected.
❑ Schools would have to produce a public action plan to deal with the criticisms by the team of inspectors.
❑ Schools could be said to be failing and placed in 'special measures', which was a name and shame strategy to raise standards.

Clegg and Billington in *Making the Most of Your Inspection* (1994) reinforce some of these points when they suggest:

> The purpose of inspection is not to support and advise, it is to collect evidence, match the evidence against a statutory set of criteria, arrive at judgements and make those judgements known to the public. Put bluntly OFSTED inspections are not designed to help individual schools do a better job, they are designed to come to judgements about the quality of the job which they are currently doing.
>
> (1994: 2)

Almost everything that happens in schools is open to inspection and it is in each teacher's and in each school's interest to make sure that what the inspectors see is what is best in their teaching and school management. The process of inspection has changed during the years since 1992 and this chapter will only be able to scratch the surface of the concept of 'improving your school' as a result of the inspection process. Much of this improvement will come from relating an action plan to the school's routine improvement plan and being aware, even before the inspectors arrive, of the school's successful and less successful areas. Self-audit is important and the main parts of this chapter centre round different types of accountability, a summary of some aspects of the inspection process and how schools can begin to find out how good they are.

ACCOUNTABILITY

First of all, let's go beyond the inspection process and look at accountability in its widest sense. There are three basic levels, which include:

❑ **moral** accountability, where the school is answerable to such clients as parents and pupils;
❑ **professional** accountability to colleagues;
❑ **contractual** accountability to employers, such as the LEA, school governors, etc.

When we summarise each type of accountability, it is important to recognise that certain aspects of accountability will help raise levels of performance, while other aspects will begin to solve the problems related to possible areas of weakness. Table 6.1 summarises both aspects of accountability.

If we accept these three levels of accountability and recognise the different and varied areas which need to be considered, it is important to realise that schools do need to work in partnership with parents and governors rather than try the almost impossible and certainly the more inappropriate route of working in isolation. Giving increased rights to parents and governors may, in some schools, make a real and positive difference to the teaching and learning process. The more discussions that heads and teachers hold with parents and governors about what happens in the school, and the more knowledgeable all parties are about teaching and learning, the more likely it is that they will be able to use this knowledge to influence what happens.

PERFORMANCE INDICATORS

Schools that are able to self-evaluate on a regular basis will recognise their own strengths and weaknesses through the processes they devise. Table 6.2 is a thorough self-audit which can be used before an inspection. The inspection process itself, which has to be the main focus of accountability, will add a further professional dimension to what the school knows from its own efforts and those of its parents and governors. It could be argued, however, that the inspection process and subsequent report is the only real and accurate test of accountability because it prevents schools from deluding themselves about their strengths, weaknesses and successes. Another way of measuring success, and therefore it is part of the process of accounta-

Table 6.1 *Types of accountability*

Moral accountability: maintaining and enhancing levels of performance
This involves being accountable to parents so that the relationships that are formed will raise standards and the recognition that if the school weren't accountable in this way, standards would not be as high. It involves written reports to parents and holding parents' meetings to discuss progress as well as providing opportunities to see pupils' work. It also involves making sure that there is a school brochure and that there are other communications explaining policy and curriculum issues.

Moral accountability: problem solving
This involves being accountable to parents in a way that allows them to make complaints if problems arise. Parents need to know how to make complaints and the action that is likely to be taken. There also needs to be an awareness of the kinds of meetings that will take place between teachers and pupils when pupils have problems in school. This kind of accountability refers to how solutions to problems are reached.

Professional accountability: maintaining and enhancing levels of performance
This aspect of accountability is concerned with how effective the school is in using, managing and developing everyone who works in it. This should involve schools evaluating themselves and monitoring internal standards and at the same time making sure that there are regular reviews of staffing, curriculum, teaching methods, assessment results and methods of planning. There is also the need to establish continuing relationships between primary and secondary sectors and to have sound relationships between schools, teachers, LEA officers and inspectors.

Professional accountability: problem solving
This includes the use that is made of assessments and monitoring procedures to discover the needs of individual children and the provision of equal opportunities in terms of the necessary provision for all pupils of whatever ability. It is also concerned with how aware the school is of its own weaknesses and how it anticipates possible future crises so that it can either prevent them from happening or solve the problem quickly.

Contractual accountability: maintaining and enhancing levels of performance
This will involve observing the instructions of legislation, opening the school to all authorised visitors and inspectors, and being able to explain and justify the curriculum, teaching methods and overall aims and policies as well as accounting for pupils' standards of attainment.

Contractual accountability: problem solving
This involves following agreed procedures for unresolved complaints and grievances and developing an effective management structure to deal with problems. It is also concerned with being able to self-audit and recognise problems that are likely to occur.

135

bility, is by using performance indicators. These are pieces of information that should help schools and will help inspectors know how well something is performing, or more controversially, how someone is performing. The kinds of data which schools can now collect to measure how well they are doing were discussed in an earlier chapter, and the measurement of performance will be the subject of the next chapter. The results of tests can give an indication of pupil attainment at a particular moment in time and also of the quality of teaching in a particular area of the curriculum.

It is easy, however, to over-value what is measurable because it does not tell us how far a child has progressed and how difficult or easy it was to get from where they started from to where they are now. However, in the context of accountability, when schools are looking at their own effectiveness and are planning for the future, they need to see performance indicators such as test scores as part of their criteria for success, as well as the fact that all those who work in the school can exert a positive influence on ways of thinking and working. The way to do this is to know what the strengths and weaknesses are and to be able to promote desirable goals for the school. This will also mean setting appropriate standards which can be linked to desirable goals, recognising the type of action that is needed to achieve agreed standards, knowing what evidence is needed to judge success and reporting success to parents, governors, the community and visiting inspectors.

SCHOOL INSPECTION

School inspection and the inspection report make schools publicly accountable and while most schools come out of the process with a favourable report, albeit couched in very miserly praise, some schools are shamed and placed in special measures. The accountability process, according to OFSTED, is to make schools more effective by the threat of failure. It is the carrot and stick method with the carrot taken away. It is hardly surprising that the bulk of this chapter should be taken up with the subject of inspection. It is stressful and difficult, with a sense of possible failure looming at the end of the inspection week. Let's start with some basic tips and suggestions that cover, in general terms, the whole of the process. The more you know, and the more you prepare, the less traumatic and the more successful you will be.

General ways to make the inspection positive

❏ *Don't take the 'They'll have to take us as they find us' position.* Use the weeks before the inspection to make sure that you are ready for the visit. This should help boost your confidence because you will know that you will be at your best.

❏ *Preparation is essential and it is never too early to start getting ready.* If you need prompts and deadlines, put together an action plan and any target dates that are necessary. Avoid the kind of preparation that means that everything is a rush.

❏ *Let everyone know what your part in the inspection is.* Getting the most from the process involves a team effort and everyone has an important part to play.

❏ *Talk about the inspection and discuss any worries and concerns you may have.* Sharing problems can often lighten the load.

❏ *Develop even more team spirit.* Working as a team will help because it will foster a positive attitude and a favourable impression, rather than conflicting attitudes or approaches. The more everyone pulls together, the more likely it is that the inspection process will be a positive experience.

❏ *Don't be complacent,* even if you have been inspected before. It is important to be equally positive this time, partly because this time the inspection will involve different people, but also because the method of inspection and what the inspectors are looking at and for may well have changed.

❏ *Don't despair if last time the experience was negative.* If you have seriously addressed the comments made in a previous inspection, you will have plenty of evidence that demonstrates your commitment to improve.

❏ *Don't get the inspection out of proportion.* Hold frequent short meetings with tight agendas and specific goals. Be prepared for strong suggestions and instructions from subject coordinators and be prepared to work extremely hard for the good of the school.

❏ *Manage your time well and make distinctions between what is urgent and what is less important.* The simple cliché is that not everything is important, and it is important to take decisions as to what is so that you can concentrate on the highest priorities.

Knowing how good you are

The public document which is the Inspection report is produced at the end of the inspection and it will list 'good' and 'bad' points in language that is less well developed for praise and which is as far removed from the language that is normally used to discuss what is happening in schools as it is possible to be. During the inspection there is discussion between the inspectors, headteacher, teachers and governors. There is no debate about the content of the report. Under no circumstances will there be any modification of the report or negotiation of the findings. The inspectors will report on, judges and evaluate what they have seen and found at a particular time.

It is important to second-guess the inspectors by recognising what the school is good at and what needs improving. To find this out, there has to be a self-audit. Table 6.2 is a long and detailed audit which, if completed carefully, will tell everyone in the school some important truths that may be found out during the 'real' inspection and which are much better to know beforehand so that the inspectors can see you being proactive in finding solutions to problems rather than being reactive and much less eager to make things work.

PREPARING FOR THE INSPECTION

The pre-inspection audit will give everyone in the school a general idea of strengths and weaknesses. Obviously, self-review should be built into all schools' School Development Plans so what a pre-inspection audit tells you should not be a surprise. If it is a surprise and there are areas of concern, you will need to work fast to put them right before the inspection. If you have left the pre-inspection audit very late, you will have to work very fast indeed. These days, you only get about six working weeks' notice of an inspection, so there isn't much time to waste, but the best way to prepare is to be in a permanent state of readiness. The inspectors will be investigating things that should be happening anyway, and not just because an inspection is taking place. No one in school, and this includes the governors, should allow themselves to be panicked into a flurry of activity just before an inspection. If you do, and if colleagues behave in this way, it is likely to be counterproductive because it is likely to leave everyone exhausted before the inspection even starts, and it will also distract people from the careful preparation and crucial matters of teaching and learning.

There are now two sorts of inspection, long and short. Short inspections are for those schools that are already regarded as the most effective. This chapter is based on the procedures for long inspections, but most of them will apply to short inspections as well. What is important to recognise is

Table 6.2 *Pre-inspection audit*

The audit questionnaire is in six parts. Each part is important and some of them will be discussed in more detail later in the chapter. The whole of the questionnaire can be used to help individual teachers and whole schools to gain an overview of their strengths and needs.

Read each question and put a ring round the appropriate number: 5 = not very good, 3 = average, 1 = very good

A. Looking at the school as a community

1. There are high standards of behaviour in the classroom 1 2 3 4 5
2. There are high standards of politeness and friendliness 1 2 3 4 5 in classrooms
3. There are effective strategies for achieving good behaviour and good relationships in the playgrounds 1 2 3 4 5
4. The whole curriculum is taught for an agreed amount 1 2 3 4 5 of time
5. Spiritual and moral development has a serious part to 1 2 3 4 5 play in the school
6. The quality of collective worship is high 1 2 3 4 5
7. On the whole, the children respect each other 1 2 3 4 5
8. Children respect their own property and that of others 1 2 3 4 5
9. There is a wide variety of out of school activities 1 2 3 4 5
10. The school makes an effort to extend the range of 1 2 3 4 5 children's interests
11. Children are encouraged to take responsibility for their 1 2 3 4 5 own actions

B. Quality of teaching

1. Long, medium and short term planning is thorough 1 2 3 4 5
2. Homework is set regularly, is linked to work in 1 2 3 4 5 progress and is always marked
3. A wide range of effective teaching styles is used 1 2 3 4 5 throughout the school
4. Classrooms are well organised for the task in hand 1 2 3 4 5
5. The work I set is differentiated and is matched to 1 2 3 4 5 pupil's ability.
6. Professional development of all staff is a high priority 1 2 3 4 5
7. Teaching assistants and support teachers are used 1 2 3 4 5 effectively in the classroom

| 8. | The learning needs of children of all abilities are catered for | 1 2 3 4 5 |

C. The curriculum

1.	There are procedures in place for monitoring the progress of individual pupils	1 2 3 4 5
2.	Moderated portfolios of children's work are kept for all core subjects	1 2 3 4 5
3.	I use the data from national tests to inform my teaching and assessment	1 2 3 4 5
4.	Assessment records are kept of each pupil's progress	1 2 3 4 5
5.	I produce an annual written report on each child for their parents	1 2 3 4 5
6.	I discuss progress with parents during arranged open evenings at least three times each year	1 2 3 4 5
7.	The school's curriculum statement and aims statement always inform teaching	1 2 3 4 5
8.	All the appropriate curriculum subjects are planned, taught, monitored and assessed	1 2 3 4 5

D. Equal opportunities

1.	Classrooms are organised to make provision for equality of opportunity	1 2 3 4 5
2.	Resources used reflect the gender and ethnicity of the school	1 2 3 4 5
3.	The teaching styles that are used do not deny opportunities that are based on gender, ethnicity, ability, etc	1 2 3 4 5
4.	The learning outcomes are appropriate to all children and do not disadvantage any group	1 2 3 4 5

E. Special Educational Needs (SEN)

1.	All the external support agencies that are appropriate are used	1 2 3 4 5
2.	All IEPs, annual reviews and statementing paperwork is discussed with parents alongside reports on individual children's progress	1 2 3 4 5
3.	Classroom assistants and support teachers are used effectively	1 2 3 4 5
4.	SEN children are integrated into everything that happens in the classroom	1 2 3 4 5

5.	Differentiation enables SEN children to have full access to the curriculum	1 2 3 4 5
6.	Appropriate training is available to help teach SEN children	1 2 3 4 5

F. Management and leadership

1.	Job descriptions are available for all teachers	1 2 3 4 5
2.	There is a staff handbook which lays down all administrative procedures	1 2 3 4 5
3.	There are effective coordinators for each area of the curriculum	1 2 3 4 5
4.	The School Development Plan is up to date and is used as a key document	1 2 3 4 5
5.	Performance management processes are in place and are working effectively	1 2 3 4 5
6.	There is a clear management structure in place which identifies areas of responsibility	1 2 3 4 5
7.	The leadership of the school is effective in managing change and developing new initiatives	1 2 3 4 5
8.	Coordinators and senior teachers monitor the standards of teaching	1 2 3 4 5
9.	The headteacher monitors the quality of teaching, planning and subject coordination	1 2 3 4 5
10.	Financial management is sound	1 2 3 4 5
11.	The governors have a strategic view of where the school is going	1 2 3 4 5
12.	The governors are regularly involved in discussions about the curriculum	1 2 3 4 5

that no school is going to be perfect, and there will be areas where further work and improvements are needed.

Documents you should have available

There are forms to be completed but this chapter will avoid those because they are fixed in tablets of stone and are provided as soon as the school is notified of the inspection. What is important, and this has already been briefly mentioned, is that you must 'sell' your school and tell its true story. An example of this is a primary school in the Midlands that received a reasonably good report, except that the reading results at Key Stage 1 were said to be poor and became part of the main recommendations of the inspection report. The inspectors were seeing the school in the light of the council ward it was in, which was one where the housing was expensive and there was a very high proportion of families with university qualifications and high status jobs. What the school had failed to do was to 'sell its true story', which was that 70 per cent of the total number of children came from the adjacent ward, which was the poorest in the town with a high percentage of adults unemployed and considerable drug problems, and that 45 per cent of the total number of children lived, despite some having high status jobs and expensive houses, in families where one or other of the parents was not the one with whom the child had started life. Both these issues, the school could have argued, would set their Key Stage 1 reading results within a different context.

Apart from the official forms that are now on CD ROM, ready to be customised, there is a pile of documentation that needs to be made available to the inspectors. It is a good idea to have an OFSTED box and to put into it all the paperwork that you think they need. You put it in and let them decide whether they want it or not. Table 6.3 is a list of documentation. It is not exhaustive.

Some of this documentation may not exist, may still be in draft form or may be currently under review. Inspectors do not expect everything to be in place, but they will expect schools to be working towards most, if not all the policies and documentation listed in Table 6.3.

What are the first steps?

Well, obviously the first thing to do is not to panic. Take things calmly and prepare to tell everyone about the inspection. There are really two main groups, the governors and the staff who work in the school.

The governors will need to arrange a special governors' meeting with an agenda agreed between the headteacher and the chair of governors. The main purpose of this meeting is to:

❑ take them through the inspection process;
❑ allow them to look through their diaries for the inspection week and to tell the head when they are available to meet the inspectors;
❑ check that all the governors' paperwork is up to date, including minutes of the full governing body, subcommittees, discipline committees, etc;
❑ tell parent governors about the arrangements for the parents' meeting with the inspectors;

Table 6.3 *Inspection documentation*

Basic information will include:

❑ Numbers on roll
❑ National Curriculum assessment data (Panda report)
❑ Attendance data
❑ Budget information
❑ Class and curriculum organisation
❑ Staff composition and deployment
❑ Details of accommodation and resources that are available

Additional documentation will include:

❑ Current School Development Plan
❑ Current brochure/prospectus to parents
❑ The most recent report from the headteacher to the governors
❑ The most recent report from the governors to the parents
❑ School policy statements
❑ Schemes of work
❑ School timetable
❑ Staff job descriptions
❑ Staff development policy and performance management policy
❑ The most recent financial auditor's report
❑ SEN provision
❑ Extra curricular activities
❑ Staff meeting programme including minutes
❑ Minutes from any other management meetings

❑ arrange for as many governors as possible to meet the registered inspector during the first visit to the school;
❑ arrange possible dates for the feedback meeting;
❑ remind them of the timescales involved that are related to receiving the report, publishing it to parents, drawing up the action plan and distributing it to parents;
❑ decide any support processes to help all staff during and immediately after the inspection;
❑ agree how the governors might need support.

It is very important to go through what the headteacher's written report to the inspectors will say. In fact it is important to do this with staff as well.

There needs to be a shared understanding so that contradictions are avoided, the right facts and figures are available and those governors with responsibility for such areas as literacy, numeracy and SEN are fully briefed. It is no good for the head and some subject coordinators to talk about how fully involved the governors are and how they play a large part in policy decisions, if the governors say that they feel marginalised and that all decisions are taken by the headteacher.

It cannot be stressed enough that governors talking to inspectors can have a real influence on the inspection outcome. It is a crucial part of the inspection framework. Table 6.4 is a list of further issues related to what governors have to be able to talk to inspectors about. This list could also be used with all teachers with management responsibilities.

It is important to reassure governors and staff that although the list of what the inspectors can ask and discuss is large and possibly difficult, no one is trying to catch them out. It is quite possible, however, that staff and

Table 6.4 *Governors in the inspection process*

❏ Make sure they have read the last report and that they are familiar with the post-inspection action plans.

❏ Do they understand the school's management structure and why it is arranged in that way?

❏ The chair of the finance committee will be expected to explain how the budget is allocated and how it is used to support the school's improvement plan.

❏ Literacy and numeracy governors will be expected to reflect on the implementation of their respective strategies and the impact on standards.

❏ The SEN governor will need to know how much money the school spends on SEN, what provision the school makes for those children and the impact it has on their progress.

❏ The chair will need to talk about how the school evaluates its own progress and development and how this information is used to move things forward.

❏ Personnel governors will need to know whether appointments are made with due regard to equal opportunities.

❏ Performance management governors will have to know whether staff development is a priority and whether the system is fair and open.

governors will feel nervous. They need to be kept informed about how the inspection is going. One way of doing this is to convene a 15-minute meeting at the end of every day for some positive and fast feedback.

As I have said, many of the issues relating to governors are also applicable to staff in school, but there are a further five broad issues that need to be in place as soon as the brown envelope has been opened and the headteacher has been placed in the recovery position:

1.   Call a meeting to brief staff and to make an initial check on whether they know of any documents that they feel they are missing.
2.   List all the documentation that you are making available to the inspectors. Publish the list and check with all staff that they have what they need.
3.   Check all curriculum policies and schemes of work, especially those that are more than four years old and those that have future deadlines. Repeat the deadlines to specific coordinators so that they are giving the inspectors the same information.
4.   Look at the School Development Plan to check deadlines. Are there any that have passed and have not been met?
5.   Set a calendar of pre-inspection events, dates and times of meetings, etc.

The role played by coordinators

All coordinators, and in most primary schools this will mean all teachers, will have to make sure that the documents such as policies and schemes of work that they are responsible for are not simply pieces of paper gathering dust in teachers' pigeon-holes. They have to influence practice and, by doing so, raise standards. If possible, coordinators have to be released from teaching in the run-up to the inspection because they will have to complete the following:

❑   Check the long-, medium- and short-term plans for their subjects.
❑   Show how they monitor their subject in the medium and short term.
❑   Discuss how they monitor teaching and learning standards in their subject.
❑   Make sure that they know how there subject is assessed.
❑   If they are responsible for a core subject, they will need to know how the national test results are monitored, how they compare with other schools and what plans are in place to improve them.

The role of class teachers

Much of the pre-inspection data will be collected, collated and distributed by the headteacher, secretary and senior teachers. Class teachers will also have a part to play. For example, they should have an overview of the school through their involvement in staff meetings and routine discussions that are part and parcel of school life and through their involvement with the School Development Plan. A short audit for every teacher, whether they have been at the school for a long time or whether they are newly qualified, might include the following questions:

❑ Do I know what is in the School Development Plan, policy statements, brochure to parents etc?
❑ If I don't, who do I need to talk to?
❑ What are the priorities in this year's plan?
❑ What are my priorities according to my performance management review?
❑ What are the strengths of the school and, according to measurable data, what are the areas needing improvement?

INSPECTING YOUR TEACHING

There are two OFSTED publications which tell schools and teachers exactly what they have to do for the inspectors to judge them as 'satisfactory' or better. They are: *Handbook for Inspecting Primary and Nursery Schools* (OFSTED, 2000) and *Inspecting Subjects 3–11: Guidance for Inspectors and Schools* (OFSTED, 2000) This section is not a repeat of the information in both publications. Everything that you need to know is in them, and if you want to adopt a hard-nosed approach it is possible to suggest that if your teaching is judged to be unsatisfactory, there is something fundamentally wrong with the effectiveness of the teachers, or it is more than likely that the children are, because of their attitudes and background, unteachable. Table 6.5 is a summary of the criteria used to judge teaching and learning from *Inspecting Subjects 3-11: Guidance for Inspectors and Schools* (2000: 6). The implication behind the criteria is that the 'test of teaching is the contribution it makes to learning'.

Table 6.5 *General criteria to judge teaching and learning*

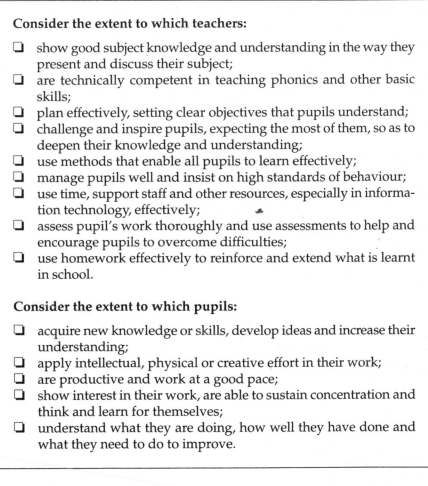

Consider the extent to which teachers:

❑ show good subject knowledge and understanding in the way they present and discuss their subject;

❑ are technically competent in teaching phonics and other basic skills;

❑ plan effectively, setting clear objectives that pupils understand;

❑ challenge and inspire pupils, expecting the most of them, so as to deepen their knowledge and understanding;

❑ use methods that enable all pupils to learn effectively;

❑ manage pupils well and insist on high standards of behaviour;

❑ use time, support staff and other resources, especially in information technology, effectively;

❑ assess pupil's work thoroughly and use assessments to help and encourage pupils to overcome difficulties;

❑ use homework effectively to reinforce and extend what is learnt in school.

Consider the extent to which pupils:

❑ acquire new knowledge or skills, develop ideas and increase their understanding;

❑ apply intellectual, physical or creative effort in their work;

❑ are productive and work at a good pace;

❑ show interest in their work, are able to sustain concentration and think and learn for themselves;

❑ understand what they are doing, how well they have done and what they need to do to improve.

Measuring success

It should be possible to examine the criteria in Table 6.5 and see how you can add them to your pre-inspection audit. What does become obvious, however, is that there are certain obvious do's and don'ts that need to be considered during the inspection when your lessons are being observed and judgements are being made on the quality of the teaching and learning that are taking place. Here is a summary that is based on Table 6.5. It is possible to link it to the measurable quality of teaching that is listed in Table 6.6.

Do:

❑ be prepared to demonstrate satisfactory or good knowledge of the subjects you are teaching;
❑ use questioning skills to assess children's knowledge and challenge their thinking;
❑ use a balance of exposition, instruction and direct teaching;
❑ use different grouping strategies including whole class, small group and individual work;
❑ show that lessons have clear objectives;
❑ manage your time effectively;
❑ employ other adults in the classroom effectively;
❑ use an appropriate range of assessment techniques;
❑ establish classroom routines which provide minimal disruption;
❑ ensure resources are appropriate and accessible;
❑ plan children's work effectively with clear objectives and identified assessment opportunities.

Don't:

❑ act merely as a supervisor or servicer of a few individuals – you must actively teach;
❑ waste time during the lesson on unnecessary administration;
❑ set unreasonable deadlines for completion of work;
❑ overuse undifferentiated worksheets;
❑ set unchallenging or boring tasks;
❑ fail to set clear aims and objectives for your lesson, as this will lead to unsuitable tasks.

Teaching quality

During the inspection all teachers will be observed teaching and judgements will be made on the quality of their lessons. This is perhaps the part of the inspection process that raises the most anxiety among teachers. In *Inspecting Subjects 3–11: Guidance for Inspectors and Schools* (OFSTED, 2000) there is a short paragraph which explains exactly what this means:

'Inspection centres on the quality of learning and of the teaching that promotes it. Most inspection time is spent gathering first hand evidence in classrooms. The central question for inspectors and those evaluating teaching focuses on whether teaching is as good as it could be and, if not, how it could be better' (2000: 6).

Table 6.6 *Characteristics of quality in teaching*

Teaching that is very good or excellent
The teaching of skills and subject matter is knowledgeable, stimulating and perceptive. It uses imaginative resources and makes intellectual and creative demands on pupils to extend their learning. Challenging questions are used to consolidate, extend and verify what pupils know and understand. The methods chosen are well geared to the particular focus and demands of the lesson and make the most productive use of the time available. Relationships in the classroom provide a confident and positive atmosphere in which achievement flourishes. Pupils are keen to learn, rise to challenges in creative ways and think further. They work well for extended periods of time and make very good progress.

Teaching that is satisfactory or better
The teaching of basic skills and subject content is clear and accurate, using clear explanation and demonstration and involving all pupils. The organisation of the lesson allows most pupils to keep up with the work and to complete tasks in the time available. Staff interact with pupils to check their understanding and to ensure they remain on task. The relationship between the pupils and teacher is such that pupils can get on with their work and know how well they have done.

Teaching cannot be satisfactory if any one of the following is present:

❏ The teacher's knowledge of the areas of learning or subjects is not good enough to promote demanding work.
❏ Basic skills such as phonological awareness are not taught effectively.
❏ A significant minority of pupils are not engaged in the lesson.
❏ Lessons are poorly planned and organised and time is wasted.
❏ There are weaknesses in controlling the class.
❏ Pupils do not know what they are doing.
❏ Pupils are not making much progress.

From: *Handbook for Inspecting Primary and Nursery Schools* (OFSTED, 2000: 49)

This theme is continued in Table 6.6, which identifies characteristics of very good or excellent teaching; satisfactory or better teaching; and teaching that cannot be satisfactory. It is important to set a more negative tone at this stage and remind all teachers that teaching overall in a school is likely to be judged unsatisfactory if more than approximately 1 in 10 lessons are judged in this way. If these lessons contain poor or very poor teaching, or the proportion is higher than 1 in 8, the inspectors will have to judge whether the school has serious weaknesses. Once the proportion of unsatisfactory teaching reaches 1 lesson in 5, it is very likely to be in need of special measures.

OTHER AREAS OF INSPECTION

The quality of teaching and learning in individual classrooms does not exist in isolation from the school's moral and spiritual attitudes and behaviour or from the outside world.

Even before the inspection takes place, parents are involved in the process. The governing body must arrange a meeting between the registered inspector and parents. The purpose of this meeting is to give parents the opportunity to express their views about the school. The registered inspector will then take those views into account and they will become part of the evidence taken by the inspection team.

Parents and the inspection process

We would all like to think that parents will give positive statements and this seems more likely if they have been involved in the school in various ways. Before the meeting takes place, why not consider your school's links with parents:

❑ Do you involve them in any decision-making committees or working parties?
❑ Have you asked for their views before and have you acted on their comments?
❑ Are they welcome in school?
❑ Can they come and talk to teachers at reasonable times?
❑ Are your open evenings what teachers and parents want?
❑ Is the complaints procedure used effectively and are you aware of any parental complaints?

❑ Do you hold meetings and working parties to help parents understand the curriculum and the school's teaching methods?
❑ Do you use parents in school to help with reading, outside visits and so on?
❑ Do you try to encourage the idea that education is about a home–school partnership?

Behaviour and discipline

One of the most common questions asked by parents choosing a school for their child is about behaviour and discipline. This may be phrased in different ways, but is generally to ensure that the school is going to be a safe and orderly place for their child. Inspectors will evaluate this aspect of the school by looking at:

❑ how behaviour affects learning;
❑ how it affects the quality of life in the school;
❑ how the school functions as an orderly community;
❑ the amount of self-discipline that is seen among the children.

These areas will be judged by looking at the quality of relationships within the classroom and the playground.

Behaviour and discipline are part of the school's ethos and culture, which are themselves part of the school's moral and spiritual development. Teachers need to encourage children to recognise the difference between right and wrong and to respect people and property. Table 6.7 will help you examine wider areas of behaviour, because it assumes that you will need action plans which are suited to your school and the kind of children that you have. It also assumes that the inspectors will also be looking for evidence of the children's concern for others and for their moral attitudes.

How well is the school led and managed?

This was looked at in more depth in the first book in the 'Primary Essentials' series, *The Primary Headteacher's Handbook*, but it will be useful to summarise some of the main issues that the inspectors will evaluate and report on. There are six areas:

Table 6.7 *Behaviour and discipline*

❑ Look at your school's behaviour policy. Does it include bullying? Does it define acceptable and unacceptable behaviour, and outline the sanctions that will be imposed?

❑ Is the behaviour policy implemented and agreed by all staff, including lunchtime supervisors and classroom assistants?

❑ Are your classrooms and other work areas such as book corners and libraries peaceful?

❑ Do the children move about the school relatively calmly?

❑ Are the playgrounds pleasant and unthreatening places to be?

❑ How do you actively promote good behaviour?

❑ How do the children react to reprimands?

❑ What is the school's attitude to verbal and physical violence?

---

1. How efficiently and effectively the headteacher and key staff lead and manage the school, promoting high standards and effective teaching and learning

2. How well the governing body fulfils its statutory responsibilities and accounts for the performance of and improvement of the school.

3. How effectively the school monitors and evaluates its performance, diagnoses its strengths and weaknesses and takes effective action to secure improvements.

4. The extent to which the school makes the best strategic use of its resources, including specific grants and additional funding, linking decisions on spending to educational priorities.

5. The extent to which the principles of best value are applied to the school's use of resources.

6. The adequacy of staffing, accommodation and learning resources, highlighting strengths and weaknesses in different subjects and areas of the curriculum where they affect the quality of education provided and the educational standards achieved.

The inspection team will judge how each individual school is performing by recognising that good schools are managed for the benefit of all their pupils and that an effective school will be one where the management and leadership create an effective and improving school where pupils are keen and able to learn.

AFTER THE INSPECTION

The period immediately after the inspection is often busier for all concerned than the period before. The first major hurdle is the meeting with the registered inspector. At this meeting there will be feedback about what the team has seen and there will be no doubt about the most important judgements and the issues for action. It is important to remember that factual inaccuracies can be changed but the actual judgements, unless they are based on factual inaccuracies, cannot be challenged.

The school's statutory duties after the inspection are to:

❏ publish the inspection report and give parents the opportunity to buy a copy of the full report;
❏ prepare an action plan;
❏ distribute the action plan to parents.

The governors are more than likely to delegate the writing of the Post-Inspection Action Plan to the headteacher. The actual writing should involve some key governors and senior teachers. This is the chance to move the school forward and to implement changes that are likely to make the school more effective. It is also the opportunity to prioritise certain aspects of the School Development Plan and link them with the Post-Inspection Action Plans. There will need to be at least one more meeting of the whole governing body because they have to approve and adopt the plan. This responsibility cannot be delegated to an individual or a committee.

In many ways the inspection is part of a cycle of school improvement and the inspection process itself is continuous in that it runs from one inspection to the next. The self-audit is also continually looping through ways that the school monitors its own successes. But it is equally important to celebrate when one particular inspection finishes, because it will mark the end of a period when everyone has been working flat out to show how successful and effective they are.

IMPORTANT POINTS

❏ There are many ways in which the school is accountable. Some of these, including the moral, professional and contractual, offer a framework within which to use performance indicators which measure the school's successes.

❑ But it is the OFSTED inspection process that is the most important. Their inspections are both judgemental and public, and are not designed to help schools do a better job but are there to judge the quality of the job that is being done at the time of the inspection.

❑ It is important for schools to know how well they think they are doing before the team of inspectors arrives. This self-audit is about knowing how good you are and is part of the process of being prepared and proactive.

❑ As well as auditing your own good practice and finding out where the weaknesses are, all the documentation that the inspectors are likely to need to make their judgement needs to be in place, and teachers, senior managers, coordinators and governors need to know the part they will have to play in the inspection.

❑ The whole process also offers the opportunity to test the school's perceptions of how good it is against those of impartial external evaluators.

❑ It is a chance to discuss the quality and standards being achieved.

❑ It is also important to make the most of these opportunities because together with the inspector's key issues, all these points will help the school move forward through its use of the Post-Inspection Action Plan and how it is linked to the school's own development plan.

PERFORMANCE MANAGEMENT AND THE SUCCESSFUL SCHOOL

This chapter looks at:

❑ performance management and school improvement;
❑ the performance management cycle;
❑ monitoring performance;
❑ what is good teaching?;
❑ what will happen during classroom observation;
❑ performance management targets and objectives;
❑ the written records;
❑ preparing for the performance management review meeting;
❑ approaching performance management confidently.

It considers the importance of performance management and the ways in which school leaders can improve the school's performance.

INTRODUCTION

Performance management, in simple terms, is about how to maximise the contribution of individual teachers to the school's overall plans to raise achievement. This will be an ongoing process and it is an integral part of how successful the school is. In fact, performance management is a key factor in making sure that the headteacher and all teachers are involved in a process of continuing professional development.

The key objective in the DfEE publication, *Teachers – Meeting the Challenge of Change* (1998), is: 'To put in place performance management arrangements to help raise schools' performance, including the systematic assessment of teacher performance linking to a suitable level of reward'.

The headteacher's performance will be managed by the governors with advice from an external assessor. His or her targets will be set at a school level and will include many issues related to the School Development Plan as well as at least one target that is about raising attainment and improving pupil progress.

The teachers' performance will be managed by the headteacher in small primary schools, and by the head and allocated team leaders in large primary schools. The team leaders will usually include the deputy head and senior teachers.

The performance management process will help the school and individual teachers in the following ways:

❑ assist headteachers in monitoring the strengths of their teachers and the needs of the school;
❑ help individual teachers to improve their own levels of achievement;
❑ help all staff to realise their full potential and to carry out their professional duties more effectively;
❑ contribute to higher standards and link with pupil performance targets;
❑ help individual teachers recognise what high quality professional training they require and how this will contribute to their own development;
❑ make schools allocate a specific amount of time for individual teachers to set objectives and reflect on their achievements.

PERFORMANCE MANAGEMENT AND SCHOOL IMPROVEMENT

There are already statutory responsibilities for headteachers to evaluate the standards of teaching and learning in the school and to ensure that proper standards of professional performance are established. Performance management is a system which is designed to help headteachers and senior managers to meet these responsibilities by formalising the process and building it into an annual cycle of initial meetings, target setting, classroom observation and review.

Each school will have different systems in place which absorb the performance management cycle. Whatever the differences, however, they should all include those statutory responsibilities already mentioned as well as effective existing practice which may include the school's original appraisal system and what is 'good' practice in terms of teaching, management, relationships with governors and parents, etc. Performance management will be absorbed into these existing areas and at the same time will add on new strategies for school improvement.

There are some key questions that need to be asked that are related to the link between existing practice and performance management. These questions will also link with Table 7.1, which is an audit of the development of performance management:

❑ How much classroom observation already takes place and how will this be increased during performance management?
❑ Does the amount of classroom observation lead to improvements and does it have a positive effect on learning?
❑ Are job descriptions reviewed annually?
❑ Is their a system already in place that helps identify professional development needs?

Auditing present practice

Table 7.1 is a method of auditing performance management. There are five areas in the audit, including:

❑ job descriptions;
❑ monitoring and evaluation;
❑ training needs;
❑ continuing professional development;
❑ teachers' self-review.

If you are interested in more self-audit methods, see OFSTED's *Handbook for Inspecting Primary and Nursery Schools* (1999) together with the CD ROM supplied with the handbook, and Smith, *Performance Management and Threshold Assessment* (2000).

If the school's existing practice is effective in terms of school improvement, it should contain the following characteristics:

❑ a commitment by all staff to raising attainment;
❑ a culture where teachers are valued for the essential part they play in pupils' welfare and the raising of standards;
❑ an ethos of trust between the headteacher, senior managers and teachers which allows critical judgements about quality to be made;
❑ an awareness that staff development has a crucial role to play in raising standards.

Table 7.1 *Audit of performance management*

Read each section and respond appropriately in the boxes.

A. Job descriptions

	Yes/no	Action needed	Who takes the action	When
1. All staff have job descriptions 2. The job description is up to date 3. The job description describes the line management and performance management responsibilities 4. The job descriptions are related to the School Development Plan				

B. Monitoring and evaluating good practice

	Yes/no	Action needed	Who takes the action	When
1. There is a shared understanding of what high quality teaching is				
2. Teachers know what is expected of their role and how their teaching will be judged				
3. Teachers are aware of the evidence that will show their good practice				

	Yes/no	Action needed	Who takes the action	When
4. Classroom observation is accepted as an element of monitoring and evaluating good practice				
5. Recording class-room observation is standardised				

C. Teachers training and development

	Yes/no	Action needed	Who takes the action	When
1. Teachers know what feedback to give to colleagues and what they are likely to receive				
2. All teachers have access to local and national data and understand how to use it				
3. Teachers under-stand what are the school's priorities in raising attain-ment				
4. Teachers know how to set appro-priate targets				
5. Teachers have all had training in how to observe teaching				

	Yes/no	Action needed	Who takes the action	When
6. LEA inspectors are used to help the school judge teaching quality				

D. Professional development

	Yes/no	Action needed	Who takes the action	When
1. There is a profes-sional development policy in place				
2. Training needs are prioritised using the School Development Plan				
3. Professional development needs are supported in a wide variety of ways				
4. There is a profes-sional portfolio in place to support professional development				

E. Teachers self-review

	Yes/no	Action needed	Who takes the action	When
1. Teachers are able to review and evaluate how well lessons are going and make the necessary changes in their approaches				

	Yes/no	Action needed	Who takes the action	When
2. Teachers are able to discuss their pupils' achievements with colleagues and senior managers				
3. There is a culture of sharing information about good teaching and what is effective learning				
4. Successes in teaching and learning are recognised, shared and used for future development				

THE PERFORMANCE MANAGEMENT CYCLE

Performance management is a shared process, which is cyclical in nature. It doesn't just happen and is then forgotten, nor is it just 'done' by head-teachers and team leaders to teachers or, in the case of headteachers, by governors.

By being a shared process it will improve good practice for everyone in the school. For this to happen effectively, everyone needs to know what the process is, understand all the relevant sections of it and agree on those sections that affect them most, such as the quality of teaching, how lessons will be monitored, and the kind of targets that will be set. I am going to assume, at this stage in the chapter, that it is more important to make sure that the whole process works. The headteacher's performance management targets are extremely important and will, because they are set by the governors, have a major part to play in the improvement of the school.

Assessing the headteacher's performance

The targets that the governing body set for the headteacher will centre around: 1) school leadership and management; 2) pupil progress. Governing bodies must set these targets and agree the objectives so that there can be a review of overall performance at the end of each academic year. This allows the cycle to be an annual one, which is then similar to that of all teachers.

Targets for headteachers can span a year or more. In agreeing them, the key points for governors to bear in mind are:

❑ The headteacher's personal contribution to meeting targets, which affect the school's performance.
❑ There should be no more that five agreed targets and no fewer than three.
❑ Targets for the headteacher should not be too narrowly defined.
❑ Targets should be related to the targets for action identified in the School Development Plan and the Post-OFSTED Action Plan.
❑ Targets should be relevant to both the needs of the school and the needs of the headteacher.
❑ There should be measurable outcomes for each objective so that all parties are clear about what evidence will be used to evaluate performance.
❑ One target should be for personal professional development, eg specific training in leadership, stress management, etc.

It is true to say that some of the key points in the headteacher's target-setting process are applicable to all teachers. It is also true to say that the organisation of the headteacher's performance management is relatively easy and that the main issues surrounding performance management lie with what happens when it is applied to teachers. The rest of this chapter, therefore, will concentrate on teachers.

The elements in their cycle will include:

1. The headteacher or allocated team leader will hold a meeting with each teacher early in the Autumn term, preferably in September. If a teacher hasn't been part of performance management in the school before, this will be to plan initial targets.
2. Both the teacher and the headteacher or team leader will review progress regularly at least once each term. This monitoring will include at least one classroom observation.

3. In the September of the following year, there will be a meeting to review achievements and to set new targets for the next year.

Figure 7.1 summarises the cycle.

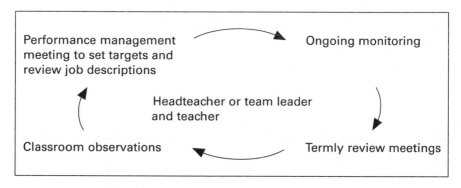

Performance management meeting to set targets and review job descriptions

Ongoing monitoring

Headteacher or team leader and teacher

Classroom observations

Termly review meetings

Figure 7.1 *The performance management cycle*

Another example of a performance management cycle can be found in *Teachers – Meeting the Challenge of Change* (DfEE, 1998).

MONITORING PERFORMANCE

In the cycle of performance management, classroom observation and other ways of monitoring performance are a vital part of the evidence that is collected for subsequent review meetings. Other evidence that could be used might include:

❑ feedback from examining children's work;
❑ monitoring the roles individual teachers play in the current School Development Plan;
❑ any previously agreed professional development and tasks from action plans that are already in place.

It is clearly the headteacher's and team leader's role to monitor teaching quality through classroom observation. All parties, including individual teachers, need to be aware of two things before classroom observation can happen successfully and before it can feed into the performance management review meeting: first of all, what is good teaching, and do we all mean the same thing when we say 'that was a successful lesson'; secondly, everyone needs to know exactly what will happen during classroom observation as well as how the observation will be discussed with the teacher and the part it will play in performance management.

WHAT IS GOOD TEACHING?

There have been several attempts to define 'good teaching' in Chapters 5 and 6. Here is a final list of attributes that needs to be shared with all staff. Remember, everyone needs to be aware of and agree with a definition of 'what is good teaching'.

Six key skill areas should be taught, because they help learners improve their learning and performance in education, work and life. These skills are embodied in the National Curriculum and need to be seen in all classrooms. They are described in detail in *The National Curriculum Handbook* (1999) and include:

❏ communication;
❏ application of number;
❏ information technology;
❏ working with others;
❏ improving own learning and performance;
❏ problem solving.

Teachers also need to demonstrate that they challenge and support all pupils to do their best by:

❏ inspiring trust and confidence;
❏ building team commitment;
❏ engaging and motivating pupils;
❏ analytical thinking;
❏ taking positive action to improve the quality of pupils' learning.

Effective teachers also exhibit the following characteristics:

❏ They ask why.
❏ They are conceptual thinkers.
❏ They have the ability to see patterns.
❏ They use data and evaluation of results to plan lessons thoroughly.
❏ They are able to analyse more and more complex situations.

It would also be true to say that successful teaching and effective lessons should include the following:

❏ a clear focus;
❏ a stated purpose;
❏ well-organised resources relevant to needs;
❏ appropriate questioning;
❏ teaching matched to pupils' assessed needs;
❏ constructive feedback;
❏ opportunities to consolidate previous knowledge and skills;
❏ high quality relationships;
❏ good subject knowledge;
❏ good knowledge of the pupils;
❏ well-timed, well-paced lessons with a clear structure;
❏ clear and high expectations;
❏ linking areas of learning together;
❏ clear expectations of presentation.

Teaching, however, will have no impact if pupils are not learning. Effective learning happens when the pupil:

❏ understands what is being taught by showing that they can do what they could not do before;
❏ applies previous learning in a new context;
❏ enjoys what is being taught;
❏ is clear about what needs to be done;
❏ receives constructive feedback which raises self-confidence;
❏ is given opportunities to work in depth.

WHAT WILL HAPPEN DURING CLASSROOM OBSERVATION

The first thing that has to happen is that everyone understands the process so that once a definition of high quality teaching has been reached, it is possible for classroom observation to form the basis of a central part of performance management.

Whatever approach to classroom management is used, and Figure 7.2 includes three alternatives, it is important to bear the following in mind:

❑ All successful observation requires preparation and training, both for teachers and for the headteacher and team leaders.

❑ There needs to be a clear understanding on the part of the teachers and the headteacher or team leaders as to why the observation is happening.

❑ Any classroom observation has to have a purpose (eg to monitor phonics teaching, to monitor the use of teaching assistants with SEN children, etc).

❑ The observer needs to have agreed the focus of the observation beforehand.

❑ The observer should be as unobtrusive as possible.

❑ The lesson should not be disrupted by the observation and should proceed as smoothly as possible.

❑ After the observation there should be feedback as part of the performance management cycle. The feedback should focus on what went well and what might be done better next time.

❑ If there are areas where things might be done better or differently, these could form the basis of future targets or objectives.

The three examples of classroom observation forms in Figure 7.2 should be freely available to everyone who is part of the performance management process. They have been designed so that the observer is able to take notes and make observations quickly. It is these observations that need to be shared with the teacher during a feedback meeting.

PERFORMANCE MANAGEMENT TARGETS AND OBJECTIVES

One of the main outcomes of the performance management cycle is for each teacher to agree targets (sometimes called objectives) which will summarise areas of priority. The targets are basically jobs that need to be done that will show that the individual teacher has performed well during the year. The targets and whether they have been achieved will form the basis of any performance management discussions during the year and in the review meeting at the end of one cycle and the beginning of the next, when new targets will be set for the following year.

There are several starting points where the targets, that is, the focus of the teacher's work during the year, are agreed:

LESSON OBSERVATION FORM 1

Subject .... Date ....
Teacher .... Observer...

Lesson details	Evaluation
Learning objectives Previous experience of pupils	Were the objectives appropriate for the pupils? (If not, why not?) Were the objectives made clear to the pupils? What assessments are recorded?
Delivery (eg timings, activities, groupings, homework as appropriate) Resources used (eg support staff, materials, texts, etc)	Were the timings appropriate? Were the groupings appropriate? Were the activities appropriate? Were they differentiated? Were high expectations of learning and behaviour maintained? Were the resources appropriate?
How effective was the lesson? Very effective/quite effective/ hardly effective/effective in parts	Why?
Have you a sense of achievement after this lesson? Yes/No	Why?
Do you feel that the children have a sense of achievement after this lesson? All/most/some/none	Why?

LESSON OBSERVATION FORM 2

Subject .... Date ....

Teacher .... Observer ....

Learning objectives and assessment Appropriate/not appropriate/lack of clarity Shared/not shared/lack of clarity Reinforced/not reinforced/lack of clarity Achieved/not achieved/partly achieved Assessments recorded/not recorded	Comments
Delivery OK/concern Exposition OK/concern Question and answer OK/concern Reinforcement OK/concern Praise OK/concern Activities OK/concern Pace OK/concern Pupils on task OK/concern Teacher–pupil interaction OK/concern Groupings OK/concern Teacher mobility OK/concern Timings OK/concern Overall structure of lesson OK/concern Marking OK/concern Health and safety OK/concern	Comments
Resources Arrangement of furniture Good/poor Availability of books and equipment Good/poor Quality and suitability of materials Good/poor	Comments
Relationships Order and class control Good/poor Attitude of pupils Good/poor Adaptability Good/poor	Comments
Suggestions for future lessons	

LESSON OBSERVATION FORM 3

Subject .... Date ....

Teacher .... Observer ....

TEACHING

Teaching input What is the teacher doing?	Impact on pupils What do pupils do as a result?

LEARNING

What evidence is there of pupils learning and making progress?

Three agreed positive points about the lesson

Three agreed areas for future development

Figure 7.2 *Three different lesson observation forms*

❏ a clear job description;
❏ achievements during the past year, including whether previous targets have been met;
❏ school development or School Improvement Plan issues related to individual teachers and coordinators;
❏ feedback from previous classroom observation;
❏ any information on pupil progress that applies directly to the individual teacher.

Obviously, the targets, and there should be between three and five, will be agreed through discussion, by the teacher and the headteacher or team leader. At least one target has to be related to pupil progress and this will be based on specific data which will include:

❏ internal assessments;
❏ national tests and/or QCA tests;

❑ PANDAS (Performance and Assessment) reports and benchmarking information;
❑ the SEN register.

An example of a target that is about pupil progress might be:

> The test results of a particular group might suggest that there is a marked gender gap in writing, with 70 per cent of girls achieving appropriate results matching teacher expectations and only 50 per cent of the boys. The target might be to increase the boys from 50 to 70 per cent over a period of a year.

Professional development

Many targets will be personally agreed and it is futile trying to list many examples, because they will be linked to specific teachers and individual schools. Examples that might be more universal and apply to most schools might include agreeing that a coordinator can observe other teachers teaching, mentor a new teacher, or work alongside colleagues in the classroom. There is little point, however, in setting targets that cannot be achieved. If teachers are to meet their targets they will need training. If they don't receive adequate training then they will find it difficult if not impossible to meet the targets that have been set. In the examples above, training coordinators to observe teaching in their subject so that they can monitor progress is essential.

The targets that are set for both the headteacher and teachers should also be based on the four areas discussed in Chapter 4. They involve four questions about the school and the teachers:

❑ How well are we doing?
❑ How well should we be doing?
❑ What more can we aim to achieve?
❑ What do we need to do to make it happen?

What *do* we need to do to make it happen?

In performance management terms, the first three questions are part of the discussions that take place during review meetings and form the basis of the target-setting process. The final question is about how to achieve the targets that have been set.

The headteacher will use the following to achieve his or her own targets but will also need to make sure that for every teacher action plans are drawn up that will help them work purposefully towards achieving what they have agreed. Each action plan will specify:

❑ what will be done;
❑ who will do it;
❑ what resources are needed;
❑ what the timescale will be;
❑ who will monitor progress;
❑ what evidence will be used to monitor success.

In the same way, teachers will also have a role to play in achieving their own individual targets. They will need to:

❑ develop a clear and appropriately timed action plan;
❑ determine the range of action that needs to take place to achieve their targets;
❑ embed the actions into a planned programme that is designed to raise achievement;
❑ understand each stage of the action plan so that purposeful discussions can take place throughout the year as well as at the end of one cycle of performance management.

THE WRITTEN RECORDS

At the end of the initial performance management meeting, where targets are set, and at the review meeting at the end of one cycle when targets are reviewed and new ones set, written records should be kept. It is important to decide whether you want to produce written records of interim meetings as well, as they may well form part of the end of cycle review meeting which, as I have already suggested, is the platform for setting the next series of targets.

These written records are confidential and should only be kept by the headteacher and the individual teacher. If the performance management process has involved a team leader, they have access to the records that they have written on an individual teacher, but there still should only be two copies. In the case of the headteacher, he or she and the governors' performance management subcommittee each have a copy of the targets that have been set.

Figure 7.3 includes examples of written records for teachers. More useful information on this subject can be found in *Teachers: Meeting the Challenge of Change* (DfEE, 1998) and *Performance Management and Threshold Assessment: Pack 1 Heads and Senior Managers* (Smith, 2000).

PERFORMANCE MANAGEMENT REVIEW RECORD
Name of teacher .... Date of review ....
Responsibilities from job description ....
....
....
....
Provisional date of interim meeting ....
Provisional date of classroom observation ....
Provisional date of next full annual review..

Areas of review discussion, including documents used, eg School Development Plan, national test results, previous targets (if any), notes from any previous discussions.

Agreed targets

1.

2.

3.

4.

5.

Staff development

Staff development and training needed to meet the agreed targets	What should be achieved when training/development is completed?

Signed
Teacher ....
Headteacher/team leader ....
Date ....

Figure 7.3 *Performance Management Review Record*

PREPARING FOR THE PERFORMANCE MANAGEMENT REVIEW MEETING

A performance management meeting is a dialogue. It is not about the headteacher or a team leader telling a teacher what their targets should be. Equally, it is not about governors telling the headteacher what he or she should be attempting to do during a particular year. For it to be a worthwhile discussion, however, it is important that everyone knows as much as possible about the school and about their own work. There are many key documents that need to be read and understood. They include:

❏ the School Development Plan;
❏ policy documents that relate to the individual teacher's role in the school;
❏ a teacher's completed threshold assessment form;
❏ job description;
❏ targets set previously, including action plans prepared to met the targets;
❏ completed classroom monitoring forms;
❏ professional development portfolio, including courses attended;
❏ assessment data including national test results, QCA results, etc;
❏ profile of children in class, including those on the SEN register.

Reading and understanding all the information that is available will help, but it is also important for teachers to be aware of both what they actually do all day and all week, and what they want to do in future. Going to a performance management meeting, whether it is an initial meeting or one that is reviewing past targets, is less productive if you arrive without having a good idea about what you intend doing next in terms of raising attainment and meeting your own professional needs.

One way of getting to grips with what you do each day is to complete the professional activities chart in Figure 7.4. This has sections on many aspects of teaching. It will be a useful point of reference during discussions to set targets.

APPROACHING PERFORMANCE MANAGEMENT CONFIDENTLY

The key to successful performance management is to see it as a positive way forward and as a tool to improve the quality of teaching in the whole school as well as in the individual teacher. It shouldn't just be accepted as inevitable, but seen as an opportunity to evaluate your own performance and to look forward to raising standards and having more development opportunities.

Staff are the most important resource in the school, and they need to know what targets are important and how to achieve them. They also need to receive regular training and the encouragement of regular review meetings. Performance management is designed to help teachers perform more effectively and to give time for someone else to listen to your concerns and your future needs.

All feedback is useful

Without impartial feedback, improving as a teacher is difficult. Within the performance management cycle are opportunities for constructive debate about individual effectiveness. All teachers need to take on board new advice and use it to develop and become more successful. Many teachers are embarrassed about being praised, but knowing what your strengths are means that you can capitalise on them. Equally, knowing and under-standing what you are less good at means that you are able to focus directly on a specific area that needs to be developed. It is a natural target and in a review meeting you will have an opportunity to discuss with someone else the ways forward.

PROFESSIONAL ACTIVITIES CHART

Work with parents and governors	Contributions to training other staff
Work connected to your coordinator's role	Contributions to team/department meetings

Non-teaching pastoral work with pupils	TEACHING	Extra-curricular activities

Personal research and study (including journals read, etc)	Work with the wider community, eg education and industry
Part played in other school initiatives, eg behaviour policy, anti-bullying, etc	SEN meetings, IEPs, annual reviews, etc

Figure 7.4 *Professional activities*

Everyone has development needs and should have development opportunities

Even though all performance management is confidential, everyone is in the same boat, in that everyone's performance is being examined and everyone is being set targets. There is no reason for any teacher to feel that they are under special scrutiny in any kind of threatening way. There is also no reason why all the staff shouldn't share their targets so that everyone knows what everyone else is trying to achieve. This is probably a positive way forward, but it has to be repeated that all teachers are entitled to total confidentiality, which should be respected, and no teacher should be forced or persuaded to share any part of their performance management if they do not want to do so.

As a final reminder, it is important to recognise performance management as part of planning an individual teacher's career progression as well as their best opportunity to discuss what they want to do and what their professional needs are. It is designed to look backwards at all those successes that need building on as well as forwards towards new targets and new needs. In doing this it is important for them not to get totally bogged down in their classroom or their school. It is important for everyone to be as well informed as possible, to read educational subjects in journals and newspapers and to attend out of school meetings. This will help everyone meet their targets, set themselves clear and realistic goals and cultivate their own professional profile.

Make sure you tell colleagues about your successful ideas, get involved in new initiatives, don't be frightened of change, and use performance management to plan your future on a personal level and also on a level where your contribution will make your school more effective.

IMPORTANT POINTS

❑ Performance management, which was introduced into schools from September 2000, is designed to help recognise the professionalism of headteachers and teachers and to be part of the drive to raise standards.

❑ It is possible to absorb the process into the school's existing 'appraisal' process, but it is important to recognise that performance management is cyclical and doesn't stop at the end of one or two years and start again.

❑ The targets that are set are reviewed after a year and the process continues with new targets that are based on how well the ones in the last cycle have been achieved.

❑ It is the achievement of these agreed and realistic targets that are the keys to school improvement, especially when it is remembered that both headteachers and teachers have to have as one of their targets ways of raising standards, improving pupil performance and raising achievement throughout the school.

❑ One difficult area within performance management that needs support and training is monitoring teaching through classroom performance. Many teachers find observing colleagues, and being observed themselves, difficult and traumatic. The performance management cycle has classroom observation as one of its key components and everyone in school needs to know what is expected of them, the purpose of the classroom observation and the use of all the paperwork that accompanies it.

❑ One final aspect of performance management is that the whole process is confidential and should only be shared between the headteacher, team leader and the teacher whose performance is being managed. It is not part of any process for judging and taking action on poor performance, nor should it be part of any other serious disciplinary issues. These are covered by other processes, and for performance management to be viewed positively by teachers it has to be seen as an effective way to move individuals and schools forwards more effectively, not as a negative way of determining and controlling poor practice.

STRESS MANAGEMENT AND TIME MANAGEMENT

This chapter looks at:

❑ stress management;
❑ the organisation of the school and its effect on stress;
❑ time management.

It considers the importance of stress and time management and the ways in which school leaders can improve the handling of these.

INTRODUCTION

Teachers often feel a sense of panic about the amount of work that has to be done and the lack of time in which to do it. Time management is of course a misnomer. We can't really manage time, except by managing ourselves in relation to time. Put the two together, however, and there is a link between stress and time management. We all know that a certain amount of pressure can be stimulating and that deadlines often have a remarkable effect on getting a job completed. In fact they can often make us draw on reserves of strength and stamina in an energetic and stimulating way. If we are under too much pressure, however, it is often the case that individuals are incapable of working efficiently. Stress may be caused by many aspects of what happens in school and at home. It may be caused by the individual teacher's own internal pressures or by how the school is managed. When this is the case, it is the duty of all headteachers and senior teachers to make sure that the demands made on teachers and the level of stress are managed effectively. If not, the school will not be as effective as it should be.

First of all, let's examine stress.

STRESS MANAGEMENT

All teachers are working in an age with greater demands made on our time and expertise. Elliott and Kemp (1983) take the view that the likelihood of succumbing to stress may well be determined by the type of person you are. They describe two personality types:

❑ **Type A** people tend to be aggressive, competitive, impatient and prone to heart disease. If anyone suggests that they relax more, by, for example, taking up golf, they will take their aggression and competitiveness on to the golf course. Such people are likely to be highly stressed.
❑ **Type B** people tend to be fond of leisure. They are not particularly hostile or competitive and are generally much more relaxed about life, to such an extent that they are less likely to suffer from stress.

It is more than likely that both Type A and B personalities exist in your school and while Elliott and Kemp suggest two personality types, it is also the case that there are colleagues who can cope with stress and handle it better than others. Gold and Roth (1993) suggest that when our 'coping' methods are successful, the 'distress' is minimised and the individual's self-esteem is not threatened, but when coping methods are unsuccessful, negative emotions are experienced and seen as threatening. Some colleagues obviously cope better than others, but effective managers will make sure that they recognise the symptoms of stress and try to explore both the working conditions and the personality and family backgrounds of those colleagues who are suffering from stress.

Symptoms and causes of stress

The symptoms of an individual's stress are wide and varied and include:

❑ sleeplessness;
❑ difficulty getting to sleep;
❑ waking up in the night thinking about work;
❑ fidgeting, nail biting , dizzy spells, nausea and sweating;
❑ nervous tics, tight-chestedness, indigestion;
❑ suppressed anger, feelings of failure and irritability;
❑ difficulty in relaxing;
❑ fear of the future;

❑ difficulty in concentrating;
❑ difficulty in completing jobs and meeting deadlines.

Any colleague or individual who has many of these very negative symptoms will have difficulty in working effectively. This will also affect the whole school and become a whole school problem. How a school can become a low stress institution will be discussed later in the chapter. At the moment it is important to remain with individuals and examine three stages in trying to alleviate stress:

Stage 1: What causes stress
Stage 2: Recognising when to intervene
Stage 3: Ways to combat stress.

Stage 1: What causes stress

There are many arguments about the causes of stress and there are obvious links between personality and working environment. Cooper and Marshall (1978) suggest that stress is directly related to the 'fit' between an individual's ability to cope and the conditions of the work environment in which the individual must function. Colleagues, together with people who are in authority, or those to whom you have to delegate work, can be a prime source of stress. It is important to recognise who they are and why their behaviour or work patterns cause problems. If this doesn't happen, it could be that an individual will be putting too much pressure on themselves and, by having unrealistic and unreasonable expectations, it is becoming too difficult both to manage and to relieve the stress that has developed.

It is also important to recognise that stress arises from personal and individual factors which relate to an individual's past experiences and perceptions. Two teachers may react quite differently to the same behaviour from colleagues. One may respond quite well and dismiss unreasonable demands and expectations; the other may take it all extremely seriously and be more likely to feel threatened and distressed. Another important question to ask is: how stressed are you? Table 8.1 is a short questionnaire that will help you recognise aspects of your job that cause you stress.

If the majority of your responses are 'O' and 'F', then there is a need to examine what you do, why you do it and what help you need from management and from colleagues. What is even more important, however, is to develop your own strategies so that you can take some control over what is causing you to feel the way that you do.

Table 8.1 *What causes you stress*

After each statement put a ring round the appropriate response:

NA for not applicable to me
R for rarely affects me
O for occasionally affects me
F for frequently affects me

1.	Feeling that I am not really qualified to do my job	NA R O F
2.	Imposing too high demands on myself	NA R O F
3.	Too much administration and paperwork	NA R O F
4.	Feeling I need to perform better and better	NA R O F
5.	Trying to resolve too many differences between staff and between children	NA R O F
6.	Supervising and monitoring colleague's work	NA R O F
7.	Class management and discipline	NA R O F
8.	New initiatives and rapid change	NA R O F
9.	Unreasonable demands on my time	NA R O F
10	Initiating new ideas and stimulating colleagues	NA R O F
11.	Having to work long hours in order to complete tasks	NA R O F
12.	Having too much responsibility	NA R O F
13.	Conflict and confrontations with colleagues and/or children	NA R O F
14.	Low morale of myself and colleagues	NA R O F
15.	Feeling that my job has little or no status and is belittled and looked down on	NA R O F
16.	Being responsible for a budget	NA R O F
17.	Attending too many courses and meetings	NA R O F

Stage 2: Recognising when to intervene

To combat stress, you need to be able to recognise the symptoms, many of which have been listed already, and decide which point has been reached on a 'stress intervention line'. This is equally important whether you are looking at your own symptoms or those of colleagues.

There are different levels of stress, with each stage being characterised by an escalating severity of symptoms. Figure 8.1 shows the line travelling

Problems and pressures causing stress	First signs of stress	Symptoms continue	Severe stress	Stress damage
	❑ worried	❑ loss of appetite	❑ physical sleep	❑ breakdown
	❑ tense	❑ irritable	❑ indigestion	❑ job loss
	❑ lack of concentration	❑ fear of future	❑ symptoms affect work	❑ retirement
		INTERVENTION 1	INTERVENTION 2	INTERVENTION 3

Figure 8.1 *Stress intervention line*

from the first signs of stress to severe stress, which can be characterised by breakdown and job loss. At most points along the line, it is possible to relieve the effects of stress, if the need is recognised in time.

It is important not to reach the end of the stress intervention line and find that it is no longer possible to intervene in any positive way and that the stress has gone beyond a point where the problems causing it can be solved. Of course, it is never easy to intervene because people will react differently to a variety of approaches and some colleagues are both unable to intervene in someone else's problem and unable to accept advice and help. There are several types of help that can be offered. First of all:

❑   Are you good at listening?
❑   Are you calm and courteous?
❑   Can you show a genuine interest?
❑   Are you warm and considerate?
❑   Are you able to focus on important issues and symptoms?
❑   Are you able to think positively about problems?
❑   Can you help solve problems from your own experiences?
❑   Can you offer positive suggestions about how you can solve your own and other people's problems?

If you are trying to step into a problem that a colleague is having along the early points on the stress intervention line, it is important to have some kind of empathy as suggested in the points above. It is also useful if you have skills in some of the following areas:

❑ **Giving advice** – This is really about offering your opinion based on your view of what has happened and what the situation is.

❑ **Teaching** – This is where you help a colleague acquire a skill or knowledge that might help them get out of a particular situation.

❑ **Changing the organisation** – If the structure of how the school is organised is causing problems, it is useful if there are ways of changing the organisation to benefit colleagues who are feeling stressed.

❑ **Taking action** – This will mean actually doing something on behalf of someone else by offering help or suggesting how there might be easier ways that will save time and yet be equally effective.

❑ **Giving information** – This will occur when a colleague does not possess the appropriate knowledge to solve a problem. Information about what to do and what action to take should be readily available.

❑ **Counselling** – This is helping someone to solve their problem themselves by exploring it and looking at alternative ways of dealing with it so that they can take decisions about helping themselves.

Stress frequently makes you backward looking, and in finding it difficult to deal with the present you might tend to see the past as a glorious period of happiness and efficiency. In order to overcome this, it is important to have a future, to plan for the long term and to look to it as a positive way forward.

Gold and Roth (1993) suggest that stress can be prevented and relieved by understanding certain fundamental factors related to the individual, to relationships with colleagues and to the job that has to be done. They include:

❑ recognising that you can't control everything;

❑ knowing that it is not always possible to understand everything;

❑ being aware that you are only able to change yourself, and this with difficulty, and not other people;

❑ not expecting to meet everyone's expectations and accepting that you will not always be liked or approved of and not everyone will accept you;

❑ realising that running away from problems will not solve them;

❑ you can never be right all the time;

❑ you can make mistakes;

❑ you are responsible for how you react to feelings, situations and other people;

❑ you are capable of change and while life is not always fair or pleasant, it is important to roll with the bad and celebrate the good.

Stage 3: Ways to combat stress

What can happen when the stress that stimulates and drives you to action and to deadlines becomes 'distress' is that individuals try to contain the stress rather than take action to remove it and to modify the behaviour and the circumstances that are causing it. Table 8.2 asks questions about what needs to happen to reduce stress. Taking the time and trouble to help yourself to cope and to manage stressful situations is time well spent. Read

Table 8.2 *Ways to combat stress*

❑ Start the day with a relaxing breakfast.
❑ Don't drink too much coffee.
❑ Don't drink any alcohol during the working day and don't use excess alcohol as a way to relax.
❑ Don't try to do too much at once.
❑ Prioritising and being better organised makes the structure of the day better.
❑ You can't be perfect, no one is.
❑ Why not come to work earlier and leave slightly later to avoid taking work home?
❑ Use a diary rather than try to remember everything.
❑ Avoid interruptions by arranging telephone calls and meetings at times that are convenient to you.
❑ Try to create a pleasant working atmosphere.
❑ If you are annoyed, try to keep calm and remain tactful.
❑ Talking through problems with other people will be helpful.
❑ Take proper breaks, especially at lunchtime.
❑ Go out of school to lunch occasionally.
❑ Make sure that you are getting enough sleep and exercise and that you are eating sensibly.
❑ Try to make sure that there is a balance between relaxation and work.
❑ Say 'no' if you feel that you are being imposed on and that by saying 'yes' you would be more stressed than you would like to be.
❑ Changing your role in school might be a possibility.
❑ Changing jobs might be a way forward.
❑ Always assume that there will be problems that are difficult to resolve.

each of the statements in Table 8.2 and make a list of those that would be helpful and that you could easily use.

There is more information on ways to combat stress in *Raising Attainment in the Primary School* (Smith, 2001).

THE ORGANISATION OF THE SCHOOL AND ITS EFFECT ON STRESS

So far, this chapter has concentrated on how individuals can recognise stress and how they and colleagues can help each other in both recognising the symptoms and working out prevention strategies. The organisation of the school and its ethos will affect the level of burnout and stress. There are certain characteristics of schools that can create stressful situations and stressful working conditions.

High burnout and stressful schools, for example, tend to have an auto-cratic management style with goals that only lead to academic achievement. They also have clearly defined hierarchies with individual teachers working alone rather than in teams. At the opposite end of the scale, however, in low burnout and less stressful schools, educational objectives are flexible, with less pressure for unrealistic high standards and an organisational and management structure where teachers meet in both large and small groups to take decisions and socialise.

It is possible to identify the following characteristics of a low burnout and less stressful and more effective school. It is important, when reading them, to think carefully about why these conditions exist in some schools and not others and how, if they do reduce stress, they can be introduced into all schools:

❏ **Trust** – There needs to be teamwork that enables the school to run effectively and this teamwork has to be trusted to work.
❏ **Openness** – Open leadership, good communication and an ethos where decisions are shared and problems dealt with in a spirit of togetherness are important.
❏ **Approachability** – Issues that need to be out in the open should be shared with colleagues, and everyone needs to be able to approach each other openly so that problems are solved.
❏ **Honesty** – If you say that you are going to do something then it has to happen. At the same time you need to know what you can do and then do it. Also, if there are problems, it is important to make it clear to colleagues that these problems are happening. There should be very

little subterfuge. Minimal window dressing and a lot of honest displays of hard work in the working teams.

❑ **Sharing** – Hierarchies often breed dissatisfaction among those who are at the bottom of the pile. Less stress occurs where there is a teacher culture of democratic participation. If this is the case, teachers need to share values, knowledge, expertise, responsibilities and resources.

❑ **Values** – An emphasis on tolerance and mutual cooperation will reduce stress because these values will prioritise positive human relationships.

❑ **Knowledge and expertise** – All schools should be learning communities where both children and their teachers continue to learn. This will mean that the considerable amount of knowledge and expertise can be shared by the whole school.

❑ **Responsibilities** – Roles and responsibilities need to be interchangeable rather than inflexible, within a loose hierarchy where each teacher feels that they have some ownership over decisions that have been made.

❑ **Resources** – All resources, including those that are human, need to be shared and seen to be shared equally across individuals and across age ranges.

❑ **Humour** – Problems in working relationships can often arise if there is an absence of shared humour and the ability to laugh with colleagues at all kinds of issues, including mistakes.

❑ **Support** – Collaborative support within and between groups of teachers helps individuals survive. Those who feel trusted and supported by their colleagues are willing to take risks and work hard to raise standards and improve their teaching.

❑ **Understanding** – Teachers need a high level of emotional understanding from each other and from headteachers and senior managers who should be seen to be interested in colleagues as professionals and human beings.

❑ **Colleagues** – There needs to be a collaborative culture in schools where colleagues' strengths (as well as weaknesses) are recognised so that they can be used to benefit the whole of the school.

❑ **Individuals** – Teachers need to understand themselves, their emotions and their possible reactions in emotional situations.

❑ **Realism** – There needs to be a realistic approach to the work that has to take place in the school. The kind of 'work till you drop' and rather over-the-top conscientiousness displayed by some teachers can be counterproductive in the long term because it leads to over-tiredness and stress.

TIME MANAGEMENT

Every teacher knows that there isn't enough time in the working day to plan, prepare, teach and mark work. If all this is to be done properly, you either have to work longer hours or do the work less well than you would like. Unless, of course, you are not managing the time that is available properly. Time is the most valuable commodity in a school's resources and how it is used is important for the quality of the children's learning.

A framework for time management

All of us can do the following:

❑ **Plan** – There is a cliché that suggests that if we fail to plan then we plan to fail.
❑ **Control** – What we do by keeping ourselves on target and trying to keep interruptions to a minimum so that returning to the plan is relatively easy.
❑ **Follow up** – This means finishing the task in hand before you start another one, or at least leaving it so that it can be easily picked up next time, or even delegate some of the work to a colleague. Jumping from one task to another is never a very productive use of time.

Another cliché that is worth remembering is that the more time that is spent planning a task, the less time we require to complete it. Colleagues who find managing their time difficult may be trying to do too many things at once and failing to recognise what needs to be done, who needs to do it and when it needs to be completed. It is never the total amount of time that is spent on a project that is crucial, but the amount of quality or uninterrupted time.

Establishing priorities

It is relatively easy to be unnecessarily busy, and those colleagues who are always rushing around racing against the clock are not always the most effective. It is important to establish priorities and then to take decisions about what to do, when to do it and how to complete the task. Table 8.3 shows tasks that have been placed into three categories of high, medium and low priority. They are in the form of a list and it may seem obvious, but within the bustle of a day in school effective time managers follow

Table 8.3 *List of priorities*

High priority	1.	Mark books up to date.
	2.	Work with the group of children that I didn't have time for yesterday.
	3.	Plan the children's book week ready for tomorrow's staff meeting.
	4.	Ring the Literacy advisory teacher to confirm that she is coming to the book week.
	5.	Get a letter out to parents reminding them of the book week.
Medium priority	1.	Make sure the library books are tidy.
	2.	Remind teachers to sort out their classroom displays of books.
	3.	Get advice on the next half-term's technology work.
Low priority	1.	Clean out the class store cupboard.
	2.	Arrange next term's outside visit.
	3.	Return call to publisher's rep re bringing a display of equipment to school.

lists of priorities. Their lists may be in their heads, but are more often written down and constantly updated.

One way of producing such a daily list is to do it every evening before you go home. This will mean that as soon as you arrive in school the next day, the list, which is ready to be worked through and amended, is waiting for you:

❑ **High priority** items need to be done urgently and quickly.
❑ **Medium priority** items can wait a short time. They are important but are not immediate and essential.
❑ **Low priority** items need to be done by you or someone else eventually. Don't leave them on low priority for ever, or they may never get done.

At the end of the day, all the high priority and most of the medium priority items should have been completed. Those medium priority items that have not been done should, ideally, move into the high priority section. As we all know, however, this is not always possible and other extremely important issues will have been raised that need finishing urgently and take precedence on the high priority list. One way of making sure that items don't get forgotten is to give yourself half an hour at the end of the week to check your lists and to make sure that any that are in danger of being forgotten either get deleted altogether because they are no longer important or relevant, or go to the top of the list for the following Monday.

Prioritising in this way is about using your time well and attaching importance to tasks. There are colleagues we know who are always rushing and moving quickly from task to task in a blur of work. The question to ask is whether they are effective in their use of time. Do they really get all the tasks they are involved in done well? Are they always efficient? Being seen to be busy all the time does not necessarily mean that time is being managed well. They may well behave like this at home too and if they do, or if you do, questions need to be asked about the quality of any leisure time that you or they have. There are 10 questions in Table 8.4. Read each one and decide whether it applies to you or to any of your colleagues whom you may be able to influence. The answers are either 'Yes' or 'No'.

If you answered in the following way, it may well indicate that you use your time effectively:

Table 8.4 *Questions about your use of time*

1. Are you always very busy on important tasks?
2. Do you always have to take work home in order to finish it?
3. Does your workload seem to be heavier than everyone else's?
4. Do you always get the desired results in the time available?
5. Are you always ready to drop everything and help out when needed?
6. Do you always have to arrive at work extremely early?
7. Do you always have time to make important decisions in a reasoned way?
8. Can you always establish priorities?
9. Do you always stick at a job until it is finished?
10. Can you plan both short and long term or are you always involved in mini-crises on a day-to-day basis?

1. Yes; 2. No; 3. No; 4. Yes; 5. No; 6. No; 7. Yes; 8. Yes; 9. Yes; 10. Yes.

Of course only Superman or Superwoman would have answered in this way. Most, if not all of us have difficulty with time in all kinds of ways and rather than feel guilty, we should be working out simple strategies such as the priority lists that will help us become more efficient and more effective. Every teacher should be working in a way that is effective and is successfully raising standards. This is not the same, however, as being a perfectionist. If you are constantly striving for perfection, this will be frustrating and more of a neurosis than a goal. Because it is largely unattainable, trying to work towards it is wasting your time and the time of colleagues. It is important to be motivated to work hard and productively and to find ways to avoid unproductive tasks.

Avoiding time wasting

Everyone as part of their assertiveness needs to be able to say 'no' tactfully, politely but also firmly. Doing this will prevent colleagues passing on to you their time-wasting tasks and your time will be saved because you will be able to concentrate on more important tasks that are of benefit to you, the school and the children. Table 8.5 suggests a few strategies that will help avoid time wasting, but it is equally important to have some more personal 'time survival tactics' such as:

❏ Concentrate and don't try to do too many things at once.
❏ Take breaks, because working for long periods without a break is not evidence of superiority. As time passes, energy decreases, boredom sets in and you will start making mistakes.
❏ Be tidy in a way that suits how you work. Try not to work in chaos but use your space so that you can find everything that you want.
❏ No one is perfect. Try to be as good as you possibly can, but remember perfection is a delusion.
❏ Say 'no' because it will save you time. If you worry too much about offending colleagues you will probably spend more time for them rather than for yourself.
❏ Don't be a workaholic. Be hardworking and give a good day's work to the school, yourself, your colleagues and your children but don't let work interfere with all the other things that you would like to do.

Table 8.5 *Five strategies for avoiding time wasting*

1. Limit the number of minutes you are prepared to talk to colleagues outside meetings. There is no need to be rude or blunt so long as everyone recognises the need to be brief.
2. End conversations that are beginning to either waste your time or eat into time that you have set aside for something else, eg 'I really can't talk now, I've got to go and deal with something else.'
3. Arrange to talk to colleagues at a mutually agreeable time rather than just assuming that they have time to talk to you. If you do this then colleagues should do the same when they want to talk to you.
4. If you know that you need to talk to a colleague, or if you know that a colleague has arranged to talk to you, have all the facts that you need available.
5. Don't just make excuses about not doing something or not having time to talk. Rather than fobbing colleagues off, promise to see them later and if possible make definite arrangements.

Procrastination

Putting tasks off until a later time or a later date is a deeply rooted habit in all of us. Not only is it difficult to change, it can also waste a lot of time. Smith (1995) suggests that the following is a useful strategy: 'Do not attempt to do too much too quickly but do make sure that you do something instantly' (1995: 204)

Delegation

One conclusion that we could quite easily reach is that it is relatively easy to be very busy doing unimportant things and that someone else could complete some of these tasks. Delegation will not save time in the overall, whole school sense. It is not about giving people unimportant tasks to do. Tasks that are delegated are important. They are planned and they are part of how the school functions effectively. They may save you time, however, and they may be jobs that someone else will actually do better than you.

First of all, delegated tasks need to be planned and they need to be identified. It is no good delegating a job that another person actually cannot

Table 8.6 *Identifying tasks that can and should be delegated*

❏ Which of my tasks can already be done by some or all members of staff?

❏ Which of my tasks make only a small contribution to the total success of the school and are tasks that a teaching assistant or administrator could do equally well?

❏ Which or my tasks take up more time than I can afford?

❏ Which of my tasks are not strictly related to my key targets?

❏ Which of my tasks are really the day-to-day responsibilities of a colleague?

❏ Which of my tasks cause problems when I am away because no one else can carry them out effectively?

❏ Which of my tasks would help members of staff to develop if they were given the responsibility?

complete properly because they haven't the skills and expertise. Equally, it is no good at all and will not improve anyone's effectiveness if you delegate a job that you cannot really let go and which you spend a lot of time checking up on. Successful delegation will mean that you don't have to constantly look over another person's shoulder. Table 8.6 is taken from Bell (1989: 164) and identifies several key issues when identifying tasks to delegate.

If it is possible to reduce the demands that are made on teachers and schools and at the same time to increase the number of teachers and the finance available, it might be possible for teachers to feel that they are able to manage their time effectively and also to have the satisfaction of thinking that they have done their job well. This, however, is less than realistic; teachers and schools are working in the present and on a day-to-day basis. They will always need to maximise their own use of time and that of their colleagues. If this happens it is more than likely that stress will be reduced and the effectiveness of individuals and the school will improve.

Looking after yourself will also improve the school

Time, like many resources, is scarce and it cannot be saved for a later date. Day *et al* (1990) suggest that good time management is about being aware that today is all you have to work with, the past has already gone, never to return, and the future is only a dim concept. If this is the case, it is important to have even more strategies and tactics for looking after time well so that the stress looks after itself.

Be realistic about working at home

All teachers will have to take work home but taking too much home so that it dominates your life out of school is not particularly helpful in reducing stress. It is important to strike a balance by only taking home what is essential and trying to get as much as possible done before you leave school.

Be aware of your strengths

Take pride in your strengths and enjoy the benefits that they bring. This will also mean recognising those things that you are less good at and taking action to try to change the weaknesses to strengths. At the same time, just because you have a weakness doesn't mean that you have to work three times as hard at it in order to keep up.

Keep learning but also have fun

The more that can be learnt about your job the better, because the more tips and experience that you pick up, the more effectively you can do your job. At the same time, don't lose sight of all the things that you enjoy doing, and make time for them.

Manage your marking

It is a very good idea to spread any heavy marking loads out evenly throughout the week. Plan for when the marking arrives on your desk, so that it doesn't all arrive on Friday.

Keep effective files, not ineffective piles

Don't spend time going through piles of paperwork to find that elusive work sheet. Establish an efficient filing system that works for you. Your colleagues will also be pleased if you reduce their paperwork by only adding to it what is absolutely necessary. Getting a particular piece of paper out of the way quickly and efficiently is a pleasant experience and it gives a sense of a job well done. On the other hand, having lots of piles of half-finished jobs can become stressful, in that they are all unfinished and time consuming because, ultimately, they have all got to be completed.

Match jobs to the time you have available

If you decide that you are going to work until 5.00 pm and then go home, do it. If you are at home and decide that you are going to stop at 9.00 pm and go to the pub, then stick to the time that you have allocated. Try not to let work spill over into every aspect of your life.

Finally, and I think that this has come out in many sections of this chapter, plan carefully, so that you leave time for yourself. It is easy to get into the habit of working long hours and feeling stressed because the job is getting on top of you. If all you do is work, you will be less effective in the classroom because you will be limiting the enthusiasm and experience you can bring to your teaching.

IMPORTANT POINTS

❏ It is important to stress that no matter how good a teacher you are, you cannot manage time. We can only manage ourselves in relation to time and if we do this badly, become disorganised and cannot complete the work that needs to be finished, then stress builds up.

❏ Sometimes stress can be productive, if it is the kind that pushes you to complete tasks and meet deadlines. At other times it can be very destructive. This is certainly the case if stress becomes distress.

❏ All of us can learn how to manage our own stress levels. Part of the answer is in using time well.

❏ It is also true to say that colleagues may also need help in reducing their own stress. This is not just extra work for other individuals with no return. Stressed colleagues can increase difficulties throughout the school and it is in everyone's interest to find out how to solve their problems.

❏ What is also clear is that schools themselves cause stress, and it is important that headteachers and senior managers recognise this and work towards developing a school where stress is minimised.

❏ This can be helped by good planning, the ability to prioritise tasks and finding ways of separating work from pleasure.

REFERENCES

Bell, L (1989) *Management Skills in Primary Schools*, Routledge, London

Brehony, K J (1992) Active Citizens: the case of school governors, Unpublished paper given to Westhill Sociology of Education Conference

Clegg, D and Billington, S (1994) *Making the Most of Your Inspection*, Falmer, London

Cooper, C and Marshall, J (1978) Sources of managerial and white collar stress, in *Stress at Work*, ed C Cooper and R Payne, John Wiley and Sons, New York

Day, C, Johnston, D and Whittaker, P (1990) *Managing Primary Schools in the 1990s: A Professional Development Approach*, Paul Chapman, London

Dearing Report (1994) *Implications for Teacher Assessments, Record keeping and Reporting*, SEAC/NCC, London

Department for Education and Employment (DfEE) (1996) *Setting Targets to Raise Standards: A Survey of Good Practice*, DfEE/OFSTED, London

DfEE (1998) *Teachers: Meeting the Challenge of Change*, DfEE, London

DfEE (1995) *Development Planning: A Practical Guide*, DfEE, London

DfEE (1999) *The National Curriculum Handbook*, DfEE, London

Department for Education and Science (DES) (1989) *Discipline in Schools: Report of the Committee of Enquiry Chaired by Lord Elton* (Elton Report), HMSO, London

Elliot, H and Kemp, J (1983) The management of stress: figure and ground, *Educational Change and Development*, 7 (2) pp 19–23

Everard, K B and Morris, G (1985) *Effective School Management*, Harper and Row, London

Gold, Y and Roth, A (1993) *Teachers Managing Stress and Preventing Burnout: The Professional Health Solution*, Falmer Press, London

Handy, C (1976) *Understanding Organizations*, Penguin, London

Hersey, P and Blanchard, K (1982) *Management of Organizational Behavior: Utilizing Human Resources* (4th edn), Prentice Hall, Englewood Cliffs, New Jersey

HMI (1985) *The Curriculum from 5–16*, HMSO, London

Montgomery, D (1989) *Managing Behaviour Problems*, Hodder and Stoughton, London

Mortimore, P, Sammons, P, Stoll, L, Lewis, D and Ecob, R (1988) *School Matters: The Junior Years*, Open Books, London

National Curriculum Authority (NCA) (1989) *A Curriculum for All*, HMSO, London

Office for Standards in Education (OFSTED) (1995) *Chief Inspector's Annual Report* HMSO, London

OFSTED, (2000) *Handbook for Inspecting Primary and Nursery Schools*, HMSO, London

OFSTED (2000) *Inspecting Subjects, 3–11: Guidance for Inspectors and Schools*, HMSO, London

Pedlar *et al* (1986) *A Manager's Guide to Self Development*, McGraw-Hill, Maidenhead

Rogers, B (1991) *You Know the Fair Rule*, Longman, London

Rowland, V and Birkett, K (1992) *Personal Effectiveness for Teachers*, Simon and Schuster, London

Smith, R (1995) *Successful School Management*, Cassell, London

Smith, R (1996a) *The Management of Conflict in Schools*, Framework Press (Folens Ltd)

Smith, R (1996b) *Develop Your Teaching Techniques*, Framework/Heinemann, Lancaster/London

Smith, R (1996c) *Develop Better Teacher Pupil Relationships in your Classroom*, Framework, Lancaster

Smith, R (1998) *Successful School Management*, Cassell, London

Smith R (1999) *The Management of Conflict*, Folens, Dunstable

Smith, R. (2000) *Performance Management and Threshold Assessment* (2 vols), Pearson Publishing, Cambridge

Smith R (2000) *Improving Pupil Achievement Through Target Setting*, Folens, Dunstable

Smith, R (2001) *Raising Attainment in the Primary School*, Pearson Publishing, Cambridge Smith, R, *Improving Pupil Achievement through Target Setting*, Folens, Dunstable

Southworth, G (1990) Leadership, headship and effective primary schools, *School Organisation*, **10** (1) pp 25–37

Southworth, G (ed) (1994) *Readings in Primary School Development*, Falmer, London

Tannenbaun, S and Schmidt, T L (1973) How to choose a leadership pattern, *Harvard Business Review*, **36** (2), pp 95–101

INDEX